THE MAKING OF A CON

Grace Larson

Published in the United States of America

ISBN 979-8-89395-895-9 (SC)
ISBN 979-8-89395-855-3 (HC)
ISBN 979-8-89395-887-4 (Ebook)

Grace Larson Books
645 Corporate
Dr, Kalispell, MT 59901
www.stellarliterary.com

Ordering Information and Rights Permission:

Quantity sales. Special discounts might be available on quantity purchases by corporations, associations, and others. For details, contact the publisher at the address above.

For Book Rights Adaptation and other Rights Permission. Call us at toll-free 1-888-945-8513 or send us an email at admin@stellarliterary.com.

CONTENTS

March 30, 1924:	Edwin Grant (Pappy) Hamilton was born in Greybull, Wyoming, to Mabel Gregory and Dr. Thomas F. Hamilton
May 26, 1924:	Pappy's father was killed by a dope addict. Pappy was sent to live with his mother's parents, Ned and Margaret Gregory, in RedLodge, Montana.
1936:	Mabel Hamilton marries Budd Johnson; they picked Pappy up and moved to Spokane, Wa. Prior to that Pappy saw his mother once a year.
July 14, 1941:	Pappy joined the National Guard and was shipped to Pearl Harbor, Hawaii.
1942:	Ned Gregory died while Pappy was overseas.
December 20, 1942:	Pappy's first conviction; He is sentenced to the Army Prison at Schofield Stockade. He is transferred to the federal prison at Englewood, Colorado. He is sent to prison for grand larceny where he served one year of a three year sentence.
March 25, 1944:	He left the US and worked on the construction of Adak Naval Base in the Aleutian Islands.
October 4, 1944:	Pappy re-enlisted in the army and left for Camp Roberts, California, where he was a cadreman, training troops.
November 19, 1945:	He received an Honorable Discharge, then left for Chicago to attend an Electronics School under the G.I. Bill.
June 23, 1946:	Pappy followed a girl to New Orleans, hit hard times, and was put in jail for simple robbery.
September 6, 1946:	He was sentenced to three years in Angola, the Louisiana State Penitentiary.

June 8, 1949:	He was released and returned to Montana. August 18, 1949: Pappy was sentenced to the Montana State Prison at Deer Lodge for forgery, where he served two years.
January 31, 1951:	Pappy was sentenced to one to two years in the Wyoming State Prison at Rawlins. The charge: writing fraudulent checks.
November 5, 1952:	He escaped from Rawlins; was picked up by the police in Yakima, Washington and returned to Rawlins.
September 29, 1953:	He was released from Rawlins and returned to RedLodge, Montana.
June of 1954:	Pappy married Dorothy Wolfe and they moved to Cody, Wyoming.
January 19, 1956:	He was charged with first degree burglary by the police in Missoula, Montana. He had another's gun in his possession and took the rap for the gun's history.
February 6, 1956:	Pappy was sentenced to six years in the Montana State Prison at DeerLodge.
February 5, 1959:	He escaped from DeerLodge and was sentenced to one extra year for the escape attempt.
Fall of 1959:	Stepfather Budd Johnson died. December 23, 1959: Pappy was charged with Interstate Transportation of a stolen motor vehicle in Savannah, Georgia.
February 18, 1960:	He was sentenced to three years in the Federal Penitentiary located at Atlanta, Georgia.
August 14, 1961:	Pappy was transferred to the Federal Prison located at Leavenworth, Kansas.

1962:	His grandmother Gregory died while he was still in Leavenworth.
July 28, 1962:	Pappy was charged with a parole violation at Caldwell, Idaho.
August 23, 1962:	He was sentenced to McNeil Island, Washington for 290 days.
March 8, 1963:	He was released from McNeil Island.
April 7, 1963:	Pappy was charged with forgery at Billings, Montana.
April 21, 1963:	He was sentenced to the Montana State Prison at DeerLodge for one year and six months.
April 27, 1964:	He was charged with first degree forgery at Boise, Idaho and turned over to the US Marshal.
August 4, 1964:	Pappy received a five year sentence to McNeil Island, Washington.
December 5, 1967:	He was released from McNeil Island and left for RedLodge Montana; then traveled on to Little Rock Arkansas, where he went to work for Lear, Inc.
June of 1968:	Pappy left for Vietnam where he continued to work for Lear Jet during the war.
January of 1970:	Pappy returned from Vietnam
February 2, 1970:	He was picked up for forgery in Albuquerque, New Mexico
March 17, 1970:	He was tried for forgery in Little Rock, Arkansas
May 1, 1970:	Pappy was sentenced to five years in Leavenworth.
April 23, 1972:	He was transferred to McNeil Island from Leavenworth.
1973 to 1976:	Pappy had his own upholstery shop in

	RedLodge, Montana
May 18, 1976:	He was picked up in Gainesville, Florida, for defrauding an innkeeper but released.
June 16, 1976:	Pappy was charged with auto theft in Glenwood Springs Colorado and served nine months in the county jail
1976 to 1978:	Pappy worked again in his upholstery shop in RedLodge
February 13, 1978:	He was charged with deliberate homicide at RedLodge.
September 28, 1978:	He was sentenced at Deerlodge.

Grant Hamilton Biography continued:

July 15, 1983: Paroled to the Alpha House Billings, MT.

1984: ended up back in Deer Lodge again because of drinking and violation of parole.

1988: Paroled from Deer Lodge Prison again.

March 30, 1994: Absconded from supervision.

March 30, 1994 until his death is unknown.

June 15, 1996: Died. Edwin Grant Hamilton was buried in the Prairie County Cemetery, Terry, Montana with full military honors.

DEDICATION

This book is dedicated to Edwin Grant (Pappy) Hamilton.

It is written in the hope that it will bring a better understanding of the inmates in our prisons; that it will foster the growth and effectiveness of rehabilitation programs to help the men and women in our prisons return to society, able to overcome their pasts and have a future.

ACKNOWLEDGEMENTS

I wish to thank the following individuals and institutions for their support.

Montana State Prison Personnel

Warden Henry Risley

Associate Warden Gary Weer

Jean Flinders for typing this entire manuscript

Almut McAuley my creative writing instructor for her support and time which made this book a reality.

PROLOGUE

When the prison gates slam behind an inmate, he does not lose his human quality; his mind does not close to ideas; his intellect does not cease to feed on a free and open interchange of opinions; his yearning for self-respect does not end; nor is his quest for self-realization concluded. If anything, the needs for identity and self-respect are more compelling in the dehumanizing prison environment.

US Supreme Court Justice
Thurgood
Marshall

FOREWORD

At 6:26 P.M. on February 12, 1978, Molly Boltz picked up the telephone. The episode that she was to hear changed Edwin Grant Hamilton's life forever.

Molly answered, "This is the Redlodge Police Department." She received no response but could hear arguing in the background. "You tried to call the goddamn cops on me," prompted her to hand the phone to Officer Craig Christie.

Craig listened. He could hear sounds of a struggle; someone seemed to be gagging, gasping, and choking. Officer Christie began to take notes of the statements that he heard.

"Goddamnit, die. I am going to hell. Mama, I am sorry. You alright Mama, huh? No, no, no, Mama, I love you. Mama, Mama, Mama. Like hell I am. I have never done this in my life. Now, I have got to find my glasses. Mama, Mama, die, you bitch. Goddamnit, die. Are you going to die or not? Die, damnit. I am going to hell, Mama."

Officer Christie heard someone trying to dial the phone while it was still off the hook. He asked for the address but this was the answer he got, "Hang up the goddamn phone. I have to call my cousin. My mother is dead. She had a heart attack." Christie then asked who was speaking. The caller yelled into the phone, "Grant Hamilton!"

Craig handed the phone back to Molly and left for the Hamilton residence at 207½ North Platt.

Molly listened to Grant Hamilton while she was waiting for Officer Christie's arrival at the Hamilton residence. Grant kept telling her that his mother needed help and that she'd had a heart attack. Molly Boltz assured him that help was on the way.

When Craig Christie arrived at 207½ North Platt, he found Grant Hamilton in the front room, standing right outside his mother's bedroom.

Mrs. Johnson, Grant's mother, was lying face-down on the floor. The telephone was still off the hook.

Officer Christie attempted to check Mabel Johnson for signs of life; he couldn't find a pulse and she wasn't breathing. The sheriff arrived at the scene and a doctor was called. Mabel Johnson was pronounced dead.

Grant Hamilton's blood alcohol content was .19, almost twice the legal limit for intoxication. His glasses were lost in the scuffle; his eyesight is 20/400 which constitutes him as legally blind without his glasses. When the sheriff slipped the handcuffs on Grant's wrists, a confused, blind, and drunken man began his dismal journey back to reality.

INTRODUCTION

Edwin Grant Hamilton still remained within the confines of the Montana State Prison where I met him in 1979. I had listened to many of the men's stories while supervisor of the inmate paint crew, but Edwin's in particular touched me so deeply that I decided to write about it.

Edwin was given the nickname "Pappy" by the young men who've turned to him when they entered prison. Faced with fear about the uncertainty of prison life, they found him comforting and thus named him Pappy.

Pappy is a short, slender man with thinning brown hair, brown eyes, and a pleasant personality. His scarred and roughened skin reflects the years he's spent in prison. His greatest prison pleasures are coffee and hand-rolled Bugler cigarettes. He'd much prefer a pack of Pall Malls but his meager budget doesn't stretch that far. The average inmate's salary is twenty-one dollars a month and prices at their commissary are the same as at the local grocery store.

I was fascinated by the circumstances which subtly but inevitably propelled Pappy into a life of crime. He was the son and grandson of prominent Wyoming physicians. Soon after Pappy's birth, in 1924, his mother left his father and returned to RedLodge, Montana. Pappy's father ended his life with a revolver placed against his right temple, in June of 1924, when Pappy was two months old. Mable Hamilton never contacted the Hamilton family again and Pappy was raised by her parents in RedLodge, Montana.

Pappy's mother lied to him about (the true facts of) his father's death. Her version was that Dr. Hamilton had been murdered by a drug addicted patient; she even elaborated the story to the extent that the murderer was caught and prosecuted five years after the murder.

I discovered the truth while researching Pappy's story in 1982. Was it his mother's secret of Dr. Hamilton's alcoholism and suicide or was it Pappy's own obsession with alcohol that led him down the tumultuous path of destruction? The secret that his mother kept, whether from guilt or to protect her son, eventually led to her own death.

This is not the story of an ordinary criminal but rather the story of a man caught up in a world within which he could not function; boyhood naivete did not prepare him for a society that inflicted stark reality.

Pappy's story is told in his own words with minor editorial adjustments. The first twenty chapters are told before he found out the facts surrounding his father's death. I am sure the reader will be as intrigued as I was by the circumstances which propelled this man inexorably onto his destructive path; a man without goals who hated prisons as much as he depended upon them.

Pappy's story as told to Grace Larson:

"I wanted to let Grace write about my life in hopes that there will be some insight into the reasons some of us lead a life of crime. Was it the first crimes I committed, the environment I was in, or could it have been my upbringing? I hope that through my story there will be at least one thing in it that will prove that a criminal is not born, but made that way through his trials and tribulations."

Edwin Grant Hamilton (Pappy)

CHAPTER 1

Looking Back

I was born in Greybull, Wyoming on March 30, 1924. My parents were Thomas F. Hamilton, a physician and surgeon, and Mabel Gregory, a coal miner's daughter. My father and grandfather, who was also a physician and surgeon, owned the Hopewell Hospital in nearby Thermopolis.

My father was killed by a dope addict when I was two months old. The man came into his office demanding drugs and when Father refused, he was shot. Mother told me the man was a product of World War I. He was wounded and Father happened to be the medical corpsman who treated him in the army hospital. Five years after my father's murder, the man was captured and sent to prison.

My mother's parents, Ned and Margaret Gregory, of RedLodge, Montana, took care of me after Father's death, while Mother worked at the Grill Cafe in Livingston, Montana.

Mother would come visit me off and on through the years but I thought of my grandparents as mother and father. They were some of the most wonderful people in the world even though Grandfather was set in his ways and my grandmother was very religious. Grandfather seldom went to church but he ruled the home with an iron hand. If he said I was to be in by nine o'clock, that was exactly what he meant.

They were both old fashioned but Saturday nights were quite an occasion in our house. Pat and Bev, our neighbors, would come over to play cards. My grandfather would get the lard pail and hand it to me; a bucket of beer cost fifteen cents then. I would go over to the bar and say,

"A bucket of beer for Grandpa." The bartender would fill it, I'd give him the fifteen cents, then carry the beer home. My grandparents and their friends would play cards, drink two or three glasses of beer, and that was the extent of their Saturday nights. Sometimes Grandpa would give me a sip of the beer but Grandma would give him hell for it so he didn't do it very often.

One day Pug, a very close friend, and I decided that if I could get beer for my Grandpa, I could get it for us too. So, I got the bucket and fifteen cents and over to the bar we went. I told the bartender, "A bucket of beer for Grandpa," and he gave it to me. Pug and I went behind the chicken coop, which my grandfather kept behind the house, and proceeded to drink the beer. We got drunk and sick! We couldn't even get off the ground. Grandfather found us right there too. He didn't reprimand us, just told us that he hoped that was a lesson. We'd already decided that drinking wasn't for us.

I went through my formative years during the Depression when a nickel was worth a lot of money. Grandfather worked for the W.P.A. as a foreman and was paid twenty-three dollars a month which wasn't much to take care of his family. My favorite dish for supper was what they called "the depression dish." It was macaroni and hamburger mixed with tomatoes; it was really delicious too.

In the winter when I was eight or nine years old, I would take a snow shovel and shovel sidewalks. I made ten to fifteen cents a walk and believe me, those were some of the longest sidewalks I'd ever seen in my life. In one day, I could make about eighty cents. I would bring that home to my grandmother and she would give me a dime for the Saturday morning matinee. It cost five cents and the other five would buy all the candy I wanted to eat. The remainder of my wages went for school clothes.

My grandfather was a fighter in his younger days; in those days of John L. Sullivan, you would toe the line and duke it out. In later years, he became a trainer and promoter so I started walking with a pair of boxing gloves on. Grandpa taught my friend Pug and me how to box.

On Saturday nights when they would have boxing matches at the local arena, two of the hopefuls would get up for a three-round preliminary and duke it out. The miners would throw money in the ring and how much depended upon how good the fight; Pug and I would get in there and fight our hearts out. We'd make four or five dollars, then they'd spend a couple of dollars patching us up. We thought boxing was great fun because we were never mad; we just knew how to put on a good fight.

Uncle Edwin, who was four years older than me, stayed with my grandparents when he wasn't in school. I didn't realize it at the time but he was very jealous of the affection Grandmother gave to me. One summer our old dog became sick. I asked Edwin, "What's wrong with Spot?" He said, "Put some turpentine on his rear end and he'll get well." I was gullible and thought that would help the dog so I did as he told me. Naturally the dog took off running and the incident ended up killing him. I felt so bad that I never forgave Edwin for telling me to do it. I'd had so much faith in his wisdom because he was older than me.

Another time, we were at the swimming hole like kids used to have in those days, and I couldn't swim. I would sit on the bank and watch everyone else but Edwin decided I should learn to swim, so he picked me up and threw me in. I went right to the bottom. To this day I clearly remember going down into that water. I could see everything. Anyway, I panicked and almost drowned before they took me out.

The only time I can remember doing anything to Edwin in retaliation was one 4th of July when I stuck a giant firecracker in his pocket and it went off. He couldn't sit down for two weeks and when my grandfather found out about it, I couldn't sit down for two weeks either.

Over the hill from RedLodge were the coal-mining towns of Belfry and Bearcreek. My Uncle Earl lived there and worked in the mines. At that time, he had five or six children so I would go over the hill to stay with them. That was the greatest thing because I had my cousins to play with. My uncle had nothing as far as worldly goods; he was fortunate to keep food on the table. In his entire life he'd never owned anything; everything belonged to the finance company.

Earl was my favorite uncle and before his life had ended, he'd brought fourteen children into the world. He always had time for me, though, no matter where I was. He seemed to understand me more than anyone else ever did. Uncle Earl's children never got into serious trouble except for little things like a jail term for drunken driving or a fight. All of his fourteen children had children so no matter where you go in this world today, you will run into a Gregory.

My grandparents raised chickens for meat and eggs. One 4th of July, I had a bunch of ladyfinger firecrackers that I threw into the chicken coop. Well, the chickens must have thought they were worms because they ate them; quite a few chickens died too. I ate chicken for two weeks after that and had to stand up because I couldn't sit down.

Up until I was twelve years old, I can't remember doing one thing against the law. I had a happy childhood, even though it was lonely, and my grandparents were very loving and understanding.

CHAPTER 2

Mother

When I was ten my mother married a man named Mitch. During school vacation I went to stay with them in Livingston, Montana. He was the kind of a person who would get drunk and since he couldn't whip anyone else, he'd come home and beat up my mother. I had never seen this type of behavior before and didn't understand it at all. I began having nightmares even though he never hurt me and I was never so happy to see a summer end, so I could go back and stay with my grandparents.

Eventually Mother got a divorce and went back to work waiting tables. She began to send money home for my care. When she did come to see me, she was like a stranger; I'd see her only about once a year. She'd bring gifts and take me places but I never felt very close to her.

When she came to visit the year, I turned twelve, she had a man named Budd Johnson with her. When she told me Budd was my new stepfather, I automatically hated him because of memories of her last husband. I refused to even try to understand him. Budd was a heavy man and weighed at least two-hundred pounds but he was a good man even though I'd believed the worst of him. My mother was as tiny as Budd was big; she weighed ninety pounds, was 4'10½" tall, good looking, and very vibrant especially when she was young.

Mother, Budd, and I moved to Spokane, Washington right after they were married. I started school in Spokane but all of my friends were in RedLodge; I think I was the loneliest kid in the world then. Most nights I was left home with a babysitter or alone while they went out; they were both young and wanted to go out and have fun. It got so I did everything

I could to irritate Budd. I didn't realize that the things I did were because of the love he was taking from me through my mother.

They had parties at the house with friends. I'd never seen drinking to any excess until then. Some of the conversations terrified me. I'd put my ear up to the bedroom door and listen. I couldn't understand why these people were so different from my grandparents. I know now that I was a very impressionable child and all of these things took place when I was growing the most; from twelve to seventeen years of age.

On Saturdays, I would go to the matinee; I'd have to take the bus downtown and back to where we lived. A lot of times I would spend my money and hitchhike home. One of those times I encountered a criminal. This young man stopped to give me a ride but instead he took me out into the country. He was an exhibitionist; he played with himself and did other things to himself that I didn't understand. I was too young to realize what he was doing but when he took me home, I was smart enough to get his car license number. That was something I'd been told to do if I ever encountered anyone who acted strange.

I told my parents what happened and they called the law. Well, needless to say, they took me to the police station so I could describe the man. The police actually treated me like I was the criminal; my mouth was washed out with soap, then I had tests and a complete physical examination. I didn't know why I had to go through all of that when nothing had happened to me. They eventually caught him and he stood trial. That was my first encounter with the law.

I became more unruly after that and began to do things I'd never thought of before. I thought it was smart to shoplift; at that time, I wasn't thinking about my future nor the effect these crimes would have on it. My school grades were okay and I got along well with my teachers. School was okay although I didn't care too much for it, but I did go.

When I was fourteen, my buddies and I took the preacher's car for a joy ride. This was done on a dare. That old Whippet had no windows but I thought I was really something driving it. I stopped at a stop sign when this car pulled up alongside of us. This guy said, "Where in hell do you think you are going?" I looked at him and must have known he was a policeman even though he was dressed in civilian clothes. I politely opened the door, then walked over to his car and got in. "With you," I said. Away we went, down to Juvenile Hall. My parents came down to get me but I had to spend two days in jail, and I was scared. All the windows were covered with wire and the doors were locked. I couldn't believe I'd done anything so wrong as to be locked up like that.

The next time I decided to drive a car I took my stepfather's car. Budd had a big Buick touring car which was built like a two-ton truck. I went into the garage, started it, then had trouble getting it into reverse; finally, I got it backed out into the street so my friends could all pile in and away we went. I didn't know it but the emergency brake was on. It was dark and we were going down the street when the back wheel caught on fire. We didn't even know it was on fire but someone called the law; the next thing we knew a police car and fire engine were chasing us. I got scared and tried to turn into an alley too fast, went through a picket fence and into the side of a garage. That was as far as I got; they took me home and my stepfather gave me quite a licking. He had to put a new rear end in the car and pay for all the damages. I decided right then and there that I couldn't drive.

My stepfather had a bottle of whiskey in the ice-box so I had to try that. A neighbor kid and I got the bottle out when no one was at home; the two of us were sitting by the heat register for the floor furnace and when we got sick, we threw up down the register. I knew Budd would miss the whiskey so I filled the bottle with water. When he came home that night for his evening drink, he knew right away what I'd done. He gave me a good licking, not for drinking his whiskey, but for watering it down.

When I was fifteen to seventeen, we used to go out to Liberty Lake a lot. My friends and I would take a couple cases of beer, get drunk, and swim. Well, I swam halfway across the lake when I remembered that I couldn't swim. I'd started to go down for the third time when a man came by in his boat and rescued me.

Sometimes we would catch a ride on a freight train out to the lake. The first time I'd ever seen anyone in delirium tremens from drinking was when this old wino was in one of the box cars. All at once he let out a scream as he ran towards us, then he dove right out the door and flew to the ground.

I paid twenty dollars for my first car, an old Model T without a top. We'd take it out to Liberty Lake during the winter and pull everyone on sleds and skates. One day the ice began to crack and the car began sinking; we all jumped out and ran but my old Model T went to the bottom and it's still there.

I was seventeen and still in high school when my friends started joining the National Guard. They received a dollar for drilling on Monday nights. My friends talked me into joining so I could go to summer camp with them. My parents were against it because they wanted me to go to medical school. Naturally, anything my stepfather wanted, I didn't want, so I finally talked them into signing the papers. We drilled every Monday night until school was out, then left for summer camp. I was in the 161st Infantry, Company B, of the 41st Division. A private made twenty-one dollars a month then, but to me that was a lot of money.

I knew nothing about the conflicts in Europe, nor had I heard of Adolph Hitler. They mobilized the National Guard and instead of three weeks training, I began my basic training to stay in the military. I could have gotten a minority discharge but wanted to stay with my buddies. Eventually, I'd have been drafted anyway.

On my first payday I went to Olympia, Washington with my buddies I ended up drunk and at a whorehouse with this prostitute who weighed about three-hundred pounds. I'd never been with a woman before and knew nothing about sex so I thought that was the greatest thing; to be able to have sex with a woman. To this day I don't know for sure whether I really did or not because she was so big and I was so small. It was really something, though, to be able to drink and go to bed with a woman.

In the Military, drinking, hell raising, and weekends in town were a way of life. We were away from thoughts of drills on Monday mornings, hikes, and everything the Military consists of.

Our First Sergeant's name was Mickey. He was an ex-prizefighter and he'd tell any recruit, "If you want my stripes, all you have to do is whip my ass and they are yours." Believe me, some tried, but nobody ever did.

I remember our company commander as a wonderful person. We would go on a ten-mile hike, and when we came back, there would be a cold can of beer for each man at the supply tent. Everyone in the outfit would have gone to hell for that man.

Three brothers and a guy named Dick were my buddies. We all went to school together, enlisted together, and were always pretty close. We went to town, played, worked, and fought together.

Later, I became close to a guy called Paul Smith although we called him, "Snuffy". He and I used to go to town together and one time while we were in Seattle, we met two girls, Eva Jane and Bernadine, Eva's cousin. A man's first love; Eva Jane was the one. No matter how many I had after that, I'll never forget her. Whenever I was with her it seemed like I was two feet off the ground. I was happy all the time and I couldn't do enough for her. All I wanted was to be with her forever.

In August of 1941, the war scare really came to the United States. They knew that sooner or later this country would be involved in World War II. The National Guard mobilized into the regular army and they told us we'd be shipping out any day. We were given a fifteen-day furlough to go home, settle our affairs, and be with our loved ones.

After my furlough, I came back to base and it wasn't long before they told us we were going to Angel Island, California, to be shipped out overseas. We knew not were.

The day arrived when we all had to board the train. Our B company and the other outfits of men started the long journey to California. We arrived at Angel Island and were there for three or four days when we boarded a ship called the Tasker H. Bliss. I think it was a relic from the Civil War but we proceeded to sail overseas in it.

The rumor was that we were going to the Philippines but half - way between San Francisco and Hawaii, we were told we were going to the Hawaiian Islands.

I was really happy to be a part of the Armed Forces. With all the men around day after day, I was no longer lonely and felt I had a station in life. I seldom thought of Mother or Budd but I did miss my grandparents an awful lot. My grandfather Gregory died in 1942 when I was overseas.

On the way over to Hawaii every time we would go down below the decks to eat, everyone would get seasick. Snuffy and I stayed on deck and slept under some P-40's that were crated up, and going to the Island with us, so we wouldn't get seasick.

The ship was full of ammunition, aircraft guns, and more soldiers than you could shake a stick at. The P.A. System went out on the way over and I made the remark that I could fix it. It seemed like they'd had many experts trying to fix it who'd failed. The next thing I knew, they had me in the radio room looking at a wall full of switches that I knew nothing about. I'd already made the remark so I figured, "Well, they couldn't fix it, so I'd look at it and say that I couldn't fix it either." I wouldn't be any worse off than the rest of them. So, I looked at that wall full of switches and to this day I don't know why I reached up and pulled that one switch. It didn't work so I told them, "That's where your trouble is." They had an electrician fix it then everything worked and they thought I really knew something about radio. I didn't know a damn thing.

CHAPTER 3

Pearl Harbor

The trip from San Francisco to Hawaii took twenty-eight days. I was one of a very few that didn't get seasick on that voyage. We were stationed at a place called Bellows Field which was an airfield under construction at that time. Most of us had to assume gun positions around the field on the beach. In the process we had to dig bases for the gun positions. If you have ever dug in the sand, you know what it is to throw one shovel out and have two more slide back in.

Snuffy and I were digging away when I said, "I sure wish I could get out of this hard work."

Snuffy said, "Why don't you pull a fake appendicitis attack?" They will put you in the hospital for observation, you will spend two weeks there just loafing around, taking life easy, and all the hard work will be over with."

I asked him how to go about faking appendicitis.

He said, "I can tell you all the symptoms and what to do; then all you have to do is follow it through."

I really went for that. Being a young kid and dumb, I'd go for anything.

So, we were digging away when the lieutenant came around. At once, I grabbed my side and started moaning with pain.

The Lieutenant ran over and asked what was the matter. Snuffy said, "It looks like appendicitis to me."

They put me in a jeep and rushed me to Tripler General Hospital.

When we got there the doctor laid me on the table, then started to push my sides.

He'd ask, "Does this hurt?"

I'd say, "No." It seemed like I did everything right because they put me in bed. They took different blood tests and I figured I had it made; two weeks of lying around, no worries, and them guys out there working.

The next morning, they put me on the table and started shaving me. I wanted to know why!

They said, "We are going to take out your appendix."

I said, "My God, I haven't got appendicitis."

They said, "Oh yes you have. We have checked and you have got appendicitis."

So, there I was. They took me into the operating room, gave me a spinal so I couldn't feel anything, but I was still awake. I lay there and watched them cut me open, hollering all the time, "I don't have appendicitis!"

There were two doctors cutting on me. This one said, "Don't cut in that direction. Turn around and come back over here where you started."

All I could think of was they were making a race track out of me.

Well, there I was, no appendix, and sicker than a dog. About that time, my buddy, Snuffy, came up to see me.

I started in on him, "Why did you talk me into anything like this?

Damn it, they took my appendix out."

He looked at me and said, "You know, the same thing happened to me." I could have killed him.

While I was in the hospital, I became emotionally involved with one of the Gray Ladies. They came in to play the piano for the guys. When I got out, she and I started going together; the only problem was, she was married. Her husband was a Chief Petty Officer in the Navy. She lived in a Naval Housing Development and when her husband went to sea, I'd go over there and she and I would go to bed.

One night, I was at her place and in bed with her. Her husband had left for Pearl Harbor but the ship had developed engine trouble and he returned home. Well, there we were in bed when he came in the door.

She said, "Oh my God, my husband!"

Needless to say, I went out the bedroom window with all my clothes in my hands. He had a gun and started shooting at me. The more he shot, the faster I ran but I did get away.

Two weeks later I met her on the street. She had two black eyes. She asked, "When are you coming up again?"

I said, "Are you kidding. There is no way in hell you will ever get me up there again to get shot at." You might say we had a brief and violent romance because I sure put an end to it.

December 7, 1941, was a day that anyone stationed in Hawaii will never forget. We had a gun position on the beach called "Old Frank 75".

There were five of us stationed in the bunker. I woke up that morning and was starting to shave when I heard firing. Everyone thought they were holding maneuvers or target practice. We never thought anything about it and I'd guess it was an hour before we finally found out we were under attack.

Even then, we couldn't understand it. "Who would attack us? What did we do?"

Everyone was running around like chickens with their heads cut off. They didn't know what to do or what to fire at. Hell, we couldn't see anything to fire at!" Bellows Field wasn't even finished then; they were in the stages of starting runways, etc...

All at once, I saw an old Hudson Bomber peel out from a power dive and come straight into the ocean. I knew then that we were at war. I couldn't believe it and didn't even know who we were at war with. Soon I found out it was the Japanese.

The next day they gathered up a bunch of us and said we were going to Pearl Harbor, to help in a clean-up operation. When we got there, I couldn't believe what I saw! We had to take the dead bodies out of Pearl Harbor and stack them in trucks, like cordwood, then they hauled them off.

There were dead soldiers, sailors, and marines all around the bay that we had to gather up. That was the most terrifying thing I had ever run into. They just didn't seem like human beings so it's hard to explain how I really felt about something like that. I was only seventeen and didn't even know what life was really all about but I sure saw the dying.

All I wanted to do was fight, and to fight them "Goddamn Japs" that did this to my buddies. Talk about patriotism, this country had it then like they will never have it again. There wasn't a mother's son that didn't want to lay down his life right then and there for this country. I was like all the rest of them because all I wanted to do was wave the flag and fight. At that time, I would have laid down my life and never asked the reason why I had to lay it down because I was so much for God and country.

December 7th there were so many rumors floating around the Island. The Japanese were going to invade and they were going to attack again. Everybody was on the alert and all of us were "trigger-happy" too. You didn't go out at night or you would get shot by your own troops. All you had to do was make a noise and someone would shoot.

They transferred us to a machine gun position right by the power plant. It had search lights and the work lights for Bellows Field. By then they were working on the field day and night. We had two fifty calibers set on anti-aircraft mounts that we had to man twenty-four hours a day. We slept in pup tents with one man on the gun at all times.

The second night, I woke up, and all I could hear were machine guns going. I thought, "My God, the Japanese have invaded the Island."

We all got up. Charles or "Kinky", we called him, was on duty that night. He was shooting off into the brush hollering, "They are coming! They are coming!"

We finally got him to stop shooting and went to investigate. Well, it was some poor farmer's cow that had wandered into the brush. Kinky had hollered, "Halt" and I guess she didn't know what "Halt" meant so Kinky opened up with those twin fifties. He spread that cow all over the landscape. That first official kill caused a war too. One poor old farmer's cow ended up on our table and one poor old farmer was very angry.

Two days later I was transferred to patrol duty, patrolling the beach at night. A buddy, Tyree, who was from Chicago, was on patrol with me.

One night a Japanese house boy was signaling to someone out in the ocean. Tyree spotted him and asked him to stop but he started to run so Tyree opened up with a '45 and got him twice in the back before he fell. We walked up and I turned him over; he had no face left and very little chest. That was the first Japanese I'd seen killed in World War II. It was hard to see a human being torn up so bad, even the enemy.

CHAPTER 4

Troubled Times

I didn't know it at that time, but I was an alcoholic. In fact, I think I was an alcoholic from the first drink I ever took.

Many times, when we would go to town at night, I'd get drunk, end up in a whorehouse, then forget what I'd done. I couldn't even remember where I'd been and a few times didn't even remember getting back to camp.

One time I woke up on Monday morning, to get up for Reveille, and found myself in the wrong barracks, the wrong bed, and the wrong company. I had no idea how I had gotten there or what time I'd come in.

One day my buddies and I were down at the beach. We'd been drinking a few beers. This colonel was out taking a swim, so we decided it would be a good joke to hide his pants. We went back to our placements not thinking about it. The next day the M.P.'s came and arrested me for theft. I couldn't understand what they were talking about; they told me this Colonel had preferred charges against me for stealing his billfold, sixty-dollars, and his pants. I hadn't taken any money; a joke was all it had been.

My company commander came to talk to me and said he was going to try his best for company punishment; that he realized that I hadn't meant to steal the Colonel's clothes and that it was just a prank. But he said the Colonel was pretty tough and went "by the book", and once he makes up his mind to something, that's the way it was.

The Colonel got his way and I ended up getting a General Court Martial. My sentence was three years and a Dishonorable Discharge with forfeiture of all pay and allowances due. I was taken to Schofield Stockade and while there I tried to commit suicide but didn't do a very good job of it. My whole world had fallen apart. I wanted to be with my buddies and fight for my country but there I was in jail for a harmless prank.

At seventeen I had very high ideals, a love for my country, and felt that anyone in power, or any of my superiors could do no wrong. I thought they had all the answers. Well, to my regret, I found out different.

I thought about my buddies and the times we'd had; we would go to Honolulu to this night club where I played saxophone and clarinet. Tyree played piano and another buddy played the guitar. It was fun for us and we got all the free drinks we wanted. Now, there wouldn't be any more of those days for me.

We were a bastard outfit anyway; by that I mean, we were put anywhere we were needed to plug a hole or man a cannon. We had no division of our own. Only sixty men returned from our outfit of two - hundred and forty-eight. While I was confined to the Schofield Stockade, I figured our company had been rightly named.

John Dillinger's bunk was a shrine at Schofield; it was roped off which made the stockade something special, or at least where he slept.

The army sent me back to Camp Turlock, California in chains. I was told I could work my way back into the service while I was there. I went to Cooks and Bakers school, and still wore a uniform although it didn't have any buttons or insignia on it. I was there about five months when they said they were opening up a new place in Colorado. A bunch of us were transferred to the federal correctional institution at Englewood. For the seven months that I was there, I worked crushing rock; we would walk ten miles, break rock down in a ravine, with a jackhammer, then carry it a half-mile up to the crusher.

After I was paroled, I was classified 4-F. My mother and Budd were living in Billings by then so I went and stayed with them for a while. A friend of my folks was a recruiter for Guy F. Atkinson Company. This company had government contracts in the Aleutian Islands and I got a chance to go on a six-month contract. Our job was to install a Navy Base on Adack. I think probably that's the most God-forsaken Island in the world; the weather changes every fifteen minutes. When I'd fulfilled my six-month contract, I returned to Billings. By then, I was re-classified as 1-A and had to report to the draft board in Butte, Montana for a physical.

I took the bus from Billings to Butte. When I got to the recruiting station, I explained that I'd been in the National Guard and had received a Dishonorable Discharge. The recruiter asked if I still wanted to go back into the service. He said I didn't have to go and could be re-classified as 4-F again, but I wanted to go back in.

I was sent to Camp Roberts, California, where I was a cadreman, training recruits. After five months, a corporal whom I'd known in Hawaii came to Camp Roberts. He knew right away and also knew of my difficulty and court martial. About three weeks after he got there I was called before my Commanding Officer. My CO told me that some complaints had been lodged against me and that I was going to have to go before a board of special inquiry which consisted of eight or ten officers. They brought up my discharge from the National Guard and asked why I hadn't said something. I told them I'd talked to my recruiter and he'd given me the choice of choosing 4-F or going back into the service.

I asked, "Hasn't my service been good?"

They replied, "Yes, you have been an excellent soldier, but we found out you have a previous record and were given a Dishonorable Discharge."

After the hearing, I was given an Honorable Discharge with all benefits due a serviceman. They told me I wasn't eligible for re-enlistment or re-induction into the Armed Forces of the United States.

Three months after I went home, I received a Good Conduct Medal!

That was the "straw that broke the camel's back." My court martial had seemed like an unfair nightmare, then the army accepted my re-enlistment, then they discharged me again, and now this medal. Was I possessed of insanity, or were they?

I worked around Billings for a while, as a bellhop at the Old Grand Hotel, then as a fry cook at the Coney Island Cafe, and at Pierce Packing.

I was at loose ends and had no real trade that I liked and could do well.

Later, I decided to take advantage of my GI Bill. I'd get sixty-five a month subsistence while I went to school so I decided on the Coin Electrical School in Chicago. They taught Electronics, Refrigeration, and Air Conditioning trades. Soon after I arrived, I found out it was a big joke; all they were interested in was the tuition money. For every instructor they had at least two-hundred students. If I learned anything, it was on my own because there wasn't anyone to help.

I tried to go to school days and work nights to make ends meet. It was finally too much for me, so I quit and went to work for the Barnum and Bailey Circus. I stayed with them in Chicago and Detroit until the season ended.

Paul, a friend of mine, was going with a girl who worked the high-wire act. She was from New Orleans and she had to go back for an operation.

Paul asked if I wanted to go back to New Orleans with them and I figured, well, why not, I didn't have any place else to go. Home was the last place I wanted to go because I was ashamed that I hadn't stuck it out in school.

We hitchhiked to New Orleans together but they were so close that I felt like an outsider, so I cut away from them and started making it on my own.

While I was in New Orleans, I couldn't find work of any kind. I had no money and no place to live so I slept in the park and bummed a meal now and then from some friendly person. There wasn't even a job washing dishes. They didn't think too much of Yankees so I was getting pretty hungry when I walked into the Buckaroo Bar to ask for a job.

A guy was sitting at the bar and he'd changed a ten-dollar bill and bought a drink. I didn't even think; I just grabbed the money and ran. The bartender called the police and gave chase; they caught me and took me downtown to the 2nd Precinct where they proceeded to beat the "livin' hell" out of me, just because I was a "Yankee". They worked me over and tried to get me to confess to twenty-two counts of armed robbery they had on their books. I knew I'd done wrong by taking the money that didn't belong to me, and I was scared, but I definitely wasn't guilty of anything else. They said all they wanted to do was clear their books and they didn't care if I was guilty or not. If I would confess, they would give me a lighter sentence. When I refused, they worked me over until I was almost a "basket case," then threw me in a cell. For two weeks I didn't even know where I was or who I was; my face was so swollen that I could hardly talk. I was appointed a jailhouse lawyer after that and taken to trial. The lawyer told me if I had three-hundred dollars to give them all charges would be dropped, so I wrote my uncle Edwin, in Wyoming. He was the uncle I'd been raised with. I told him of my situation and that I didn't want my folks or grandmother to know; it would have broken my grandmother's heart. I asked him, "Please help me." I knew he could because he did have enough money. He and his wife had a cafe in Rock Springs.

Well, I received a letter back that said, "I and my wife have decided that you should face up to your acts and take your punishment. Therefore, we are sending no money."

CHAPTER 5

Angola Hell on Earth

They sentenced me to three years in Angola beginning September 6, 1946, and ending June 8th, 1949. They gave me credit for the time I'd spent in jail. At that time, I had no idea what the name Angola meant. If I'd known it was another name for Hell, I think I would have tried to do away with myself.

I was taken in chains to their prison farm called Angola. It was 27,000 acres of sugar cane fields with camps for blacks and camps for whites.

When I came in the front door of what they called the "Big House", which was like a plantation house, the head man said, "Boy, you see all that land out there?" I said, "Yes, Sir." He said, "Well, that's my land and that's your cane. Now get your fuckin' cane off my land."

That was my first experience at a penitentiary and I couldn't believe that anything like this existed on this earth; anything so brutal and sadistic.

The long hours, wearing stripes, and starvation was just like the old chain gangs. They beat us with leather whips and had convict guards. I thought the Germans and Japanese were cruel in World War II, but they were nothing compared to what we had in this country.

I am talking about Angola because I feel it was the turning point in my life. But in order for you to understand, you would have to understand how I was then. I was very young, twenty-one, still a green kid, and I didn't know much about life. Homosexuals, I didn't even know what they were!

Narcotics and marijuana were almost unheard of and I had no idea how to use them or even what they were.

On the prison farm were camps; H camp was for first timers and E camp was for losers and hardcore. There were four or five camps that were all colored people and then a women's camp, where the colored and white women were separated. The white girls worked in the Free People's houses as maids and servants. One white girl worked for the Catholic priest and one worked for the Protestant chaplain. The priest and the chaplain were both alcoholics. Of course, every six months or so, they would have to change maids because in some strange way those girls became pregnant.

If a man went to either the priest or the chaplain seeking spiritual guidance or help, all he got was to "Get the hell out" because they had nothing for you. They were the poorest excuse for men of religion I have ever seen in my life!

No doubt you have seen movies about chain gangs, read books, and heard stories but they were nothing compared to the real thing. When I arrived there, I was dressed out in a pair of pants with ring-tailed stripes and a shirt to match. Then they gave me a spoon which was my only eating utensil; I was to keep it for as long as I was there because I'd never be given another one.

The Free Man at the big house told me, "There are two things we have no use for down here. One is a Nigger and the other is a Yankee. Now a Nigger is just a little bit better than a Yankee. From now on you will be called, "The Four-Eyed Yankee". I was then taken out and put on the back of a truck with two convict guards. They took me to Camp H; my first stop in Hell.

Camp H consisted of a cement building surrounded by barbed wire and gun towers like a concentration camp. Upstairs was a big dorm and downstairs was the mess hall. My second night at Camp H, the bully of the camp thought he was going to have himself a new "kid". He and I got into a fight and I ran his head through a glass window cutting him up pretty bad. So, they decided I was hardcore even though I was a first timer.

They bundled me up and sent me to Camp E which was the same as Camp H except it had a butcher shop and a mess hall on the ground floor. I guess they figured hardcores were better in the butcher trade.

Off the main building was a barber shop so whenever we wanted a shave we went in, checked out a razor and shaved. The ones that had money or political pull were able to have the service of a barber. There were many favors to be had in that camp if you had the money.

The camp was run by a captain called the Camp Captain and a few free men. It was guarded by convict guards and when I say convict guards, I mean men that were doing life or one to two hundred years. They would give them a rifle or shotgun, put them in khakis and tell them that if someone tried to escape, if they shot him, they'd be given time off their sentences. A man doing time, if he kept on his toes, would be out before long because all he had to do was kill a few people.

This may sound rather harsh but that place had its own coroner and doctor. No matter how people died, all they would put on the death certificate was sunstroke. It didn't matter if they were stabbed, committed suicide, were shot or died of a heart attack while working in the fields. There was no other death but sunstroke in that place.

The food was grits and gravy in the morning, red beans and rice at noon, okra with cornbread at night and it was starvation food. If you didn't have money that is what you had all the time you were there. I was hungry all of the time and they never served pie or cake; things we take for granted were non-existent. Once in a while we had biscuits which we called "cat heads" and cream gravy for breakfast. That was usually the best meal.

Upstairs in the dorm we were crowded in three bunks high and six bunks together. I would have to climb over three bunks to get to mine and we were packed in like sardines. We were awakened each morning with a hammer beating on a steel door then sent to the mess hall to eat out of our pie tin with our only spoon. When they decided that we'd had enough, they would ring the bell that hung in the mess hall and open the doors. Free men stood on each side of the doors with long brass-ended hickory sticks waiting to whip the last men out. When the bell rang, everybody would take off, over and around tables any way they could get out of those doors, running over each other just like a crowd when someone yells, "Fire", or like a bunch of animals turned loose all at once.

We would form out in the yard, two to three hundred men, and they would take sick call. Believe me, if you reported for sick call, you had better be sick, running a temperature of 102 or 103, because if you were just malingering you would be sick before the day was done. Now I know this because I went through it. They had two posts in the yard with two leather straps hanging from a crossbeam, and those straps fit around a man's wrists. I reported for sick call and wasn't sick so they took me to the yard, put those straps on my wrists and hung me up so my toes could barely touch the ground. Then they came out with a glass of castor oil and the hot sun worked on me and I just shit all over myself. They left me there until quitting time which was sundown, then I was taken down so I could go in and take a bath. By then I was so weak I could barely stand up. I decided right then and there that I'd never go on sick call again. They would have to carry me to the hospital first.

The morning I went to work, they formed a line of about 150 men. We were marched out of the compound with convict guards on each side and a free man, like a field foreman, on a big white horse following in the rear. We marched four or five miles to our work site which was a sugar cane field.

They lined us up, one man to a row. One man was called a lead man and he'd set the pace for us to work on the rows. There were guards on the section we were working and the free man rode behind us on his horse.

The free man's name was Quinn. This man was big, fat, coarse talking and illiterate, almost stupid, and we called him the "Hook n' Bull". His horse's name was Satan which was very appropriate because he would bite or walk over us if we didn't get out of his way.

We'd start up those rows with sugar cane knives, similar to a machete, only they had a hook on the end to strip the leaves off the sugar cane tops. We would top the sugar cane, strip it, drop it and keep right on going up one row and down the other all day without rest.

At noon they would bring us beans to eat. We had to manage eating those beans within thirty minutes and if it rained, we just had more beans to eat because we couldn't get out of the rain.

Our bodies were crisscrossed with scratches from the sharp sugar cane leaves. We didn't have a shirt to wear and sweat would run into those scratches and make it pretty damn miserable.

The first day on the job I started out with my knife but since I didn't know how to use it, the first thing I did was run that hook into my leg and cut it. I threw that goddamned knife down and said, "I'm not going to cut no sugar cane." The Hook n' Bull came up and said, "What did you say, boy?" I said, "I ain't cutting anymore of your fuckin' sugar cane!"

He told two of the guards, "Spread eagle that boy on the headland. Let's teach that Yankee a lesson." Three of them got me and laid me down, then the boss got off his horse and proceeded to work me over with his "cat 'o nine tails". They put the knife back in my hand and let me up. After fifteen or so licks of that cat 'o nine tails I learned to cut sugar cane and became one of the best cutters they had.

When we went in that night, my pants were stuck to my legs and rear end because of the dried blood from that beating. A buddy of mine had to soak my pants so he could get them loose from my skin.

I acquired two very good friends while I was in Angola. One was Bob Ashley who was also my work partner. We were called the two little Yankees because he was from Indiana and I was from Montana. Bob was my size, 5'7", and heavy set with brown hair and blue eyes. His dad was doing time for bank robbery. I guess Bob learned from him, Clair Fenler was tall, fair, and good looking. He was Italian and had a beautiful head of wavy brown hair. He, Bob, and I ate together, worked together, and our bunks were side by side. I was 22 and Bob and Clair were close to my age or in their mid-twenties.

Bunking together was a mutual protection thing because we were all so young. More than once, we came in at night and found a letter from some old pervert that wanted a "kid". Physically, we were never bothered although many of the weaker men were. They could not take the sugar cane or the starvation rations so they would sell themselves to be used sexually to escape the other evils.

There were some light moments there. I remember the time we were working out in the vegetable garden picking tomatoes. We didn't dare eat one of those tomatoes because if we were seen we'd get our heads beat in. I picked this big juicy tomato and it looked so delicious, ripened just right and big enough for a meal. The boss was riding up ahead on Satan and before I knew what I was doing, I drew back and threw that tomato. It hit him in the back of the head and splattered all over. He wheeled Satan around and came back. I thought, "Oh, Lord, I'm going to get my head whipped now." But he kept right on going and stopped by Bob Ashley whipping him over the head about five times.

When we got back to camp that night Bob said, "God damn you, you can get me into more goddamned trouble than any guy I know." In a way we thought it was funny because there was no harm done, just a few lumps here and there and we were accustomed to lumps.

Another time, I cut the cinch on old Satan's saddle most of the way through. When we'd move up in the fields the Hook n' Bull would jump the ditches on Satan, and the rest of us would walk around. When Satan jumped that ditch, the cinch broke. The Hook n' Bull fell off in the mud but luckily for me, he never found out who did it.

CHAPTER 6

The Long Line

I spent practically all my time in the Long Line cutting sugar cane for the Hook n' Bull. He was so sadistic that I think the man was mentally unbalanced. I saw him get so mad that he'd get down off his horse, throw his hat on the ground, then take a club and beat himself on the head with it.

There were about a hundred of us in the Long Line who marched by the Hook n' Bull's house, on our way to the field. The man's two daughters would be out on the porch and he'd holler at them, "You goddamned whores, get in the house. There ain't none of these boys gonna fuck you!" Now isn't that a hell of a way for a man to talk to his daughters but that's the way he was.

The Hook n' Bull couldn't read or write his own name. I saw them bring his check to him. He'd sit up there on that big, white horse looking at that check, take out his pen, and very elaborately like he was really doing something, make a big X.

He'd tell a man that his mother was a whore, his father a pimp, or that the man was just no good. The Hook n' Bull would constantly ride a man, just hoping he'd try something, so he could beat him or have one of the convict guards shoot him.

Whenever we had to go to the bathroom out in the field, we'd holler "Gettin' down, Boss!" When we had permission, we could go over to the "shit ditch" and do what we had to do. After we were through, we had to get a stick and bring a little bit back to show the Hook n' Bull, to prove we weren't goofing off but really had to go.

Two brothers came to work in the fields; they rode horses and ran the long line. One day a thunder storm came up with lightening striking one of them and his horse. Whenever we'd have the surviving brother for our boss, and it would start clouding up with a little thunder, everyone would holler, "Strike him dead, Jesus!" Well, when we said that, he would take us all in to the house. I guess he figured all that praying must be heard and he didn't want to be out there or the old Lord would strike him too. And we were hoping He would strike him because it was our only salvation.

One day, they came and took me out of the field and put me in the Blacksmith Shop. I couldn't figure out how come I was lucky enough to get such an easy job. Well, it didn't take long to find out; the Blacksmith, who was also a convict, wanted my body. When I found that out, I went back to the Long Line.

The next break for me was working in the barn taking care of the mules and horses. We had two mules, one named Tony, and a female mule. Tony was meaner than hell.

Occasionally negro women would work in the field next to us. We would give one of the convict guards two dollars, he'd give the free man one dollar, keep fifty cents for himself, and give the girl fifty cents. Then we could take the women down in the ditches and take care of our natural urges. The girls were glad to make fifty cents and everyone was happy. That was one of the highlights of my stay in Angola.

One of the men on the Long Line was a bully and I guess he decided that I was fair meat. He tried to put his work on me all the time, hoping that I'd break, but I never did.

One day we were out cutting ditch banks with our scythes. We would swing the blade in a circle cutting grass from the sides of the banks. I was the last one in line going up the bank and the bully was leaving his work for me. This had been going on for a month or more and I'd had enough of it. The guys stopped for a break and I kept right on cutting. When I got up to the bully, I swung the blade cutting him across the throat. I had intended to kill him because I figured that was the only way I could get him off my back. They put him in a truck, took him to the hospital and sewed him up.

I said it was an accident, that I hadn't realized that they'd stopped for a break, and kept right on cutting. They couldn't prove otherwise so nothing happened, but I got him off my back and gained the respect of the entire crew. Nobody bothered me after that. They knew that before I would submit, I'd either kill them or myself.

They took Clair Fensler from the fields to work in the records department. Clair had a college education and that meant a lot, because most of the free men who worked there couldn't read or write.

We'd see Clair every night and he'd tell us how good it was at the Big House. He also said he was going to escape and told Bob and I how he was going to do it and where he was going to hide the first night, so he could leave. He really thought he could get away from there.

The next day, the guards searched the whole place and couldn't find him. They knew the three of us were friends so first Bob was called in to see what he knew about it. If he would tell, they would make him a convict guard. That was like a death sentence because the convict guards had to be kept away from the other convicts or they'd be murdered. Bob declined their offer as he sure didn't want to be a convict guard. Besides, we had a code that nobody told on anyone else, and every man protects the other man. They even offered him parole. When he still wouldn't tell, they beat the hell out of him and that didn't do any good either.

I was next and believe me if a man ever wanted out of a place, God knows I did, but I refused to tell them anything. They worked me over, and I'm one of those people who, the more I'm beaten, the more stubborn I get. I wouldn't have told them if they'd beaten me to death so they sent me back to camp.

Four days later they found poor Clair. Angola sits, like in a horseshoe, with the Mississippi River around it and twenty miles of swamp after that, to go through. Not knowing the country, Clair was caught out in the swamps.

People on sharecropping farms knew there was a fifty-dollar reward for any convict who escaped and fifty dollars was a lot of money to them. We couldn't really blame them for turning Clair in because they were starving to death, trying to make it on a hard scrabble farm. I don't remember anyone holding animosity towards them for what they did. There were a few instances where some of them had actually helped a convict get away. They knew how bad that place was and some of them had been in there.

During the harvest, a lot of us worked in the sugar cane mill where the cane was processed into brown sugar. It was sold to a sugar company in Louisiana and trucked from the sugar mill. I worked in the mill as a bench chemist. That was a break and I really enjoyed it; it was the only job that I liked during my time in Angola.

At the end of each year the convicts would get five dollars for that year's work. That five dollars meant an awful lot to us. There would be all kinds of gambling; card games, dice games, and a few convicts would end up with all the money, but we had a hell of a time while it lasted. We'd get a few days off for Christmas so that was our time of the year. They didn't recognize the 4th of July or any of the holidays that they do now in these places. That was our only time to rest.

CHAPTER 7

Human Savages

We were allowed to have money if we had it sent in but the camp captain took his share. If we got twenty, he took five, and gave us fifteen. We could carry that with us, buy little things, play poker, and shoot craps. An old man named Charlie ran the poker tables. He was about the same age I am now, fifty-eight, and had a desire for young boys. Charlie was tall and skinny with a friendly way, especially for anyone who was young. His occupation had been robbing banks. Charlie had the death sentence waiting for him in Texas and Mississippi as well as two-hundred and eighty-seven years to serve in Angola. He knew he'd never live long enough to get out. I guess he was one of the original bad men as he'd killed a few prison guards while trying to escape; he'd even killed a few in Angola. Charlie always had quite a bit of money and he used narcotics pretty heavy but he was a good old soul.

Occasionally I worked the poker tables for Charlie. He would stake me to begin with then give me a percentage of my winnings. One night a guy named Lime Eater came staggering past my table with blood pouring from at least eight stab wounds. I looked up and froze. That was the first time I'd seen anything like that so I looked around to see what the other players were going to do. They went right on playing cards as if nothing had happened so I went back to my cards. Lime Eater made it as far as the door and fell over dead. He lay there all night before they finally came and got him. That was the first person I'd seen killed there.

We had it fairly easy compared to the negroes because they would kill one of them about once a week. One of the old camp captains had a love affair with a divorcee and his wife was in the way, so he killed his wife and blamed it on their negro houseboy. Well, they got out the dogs and went looking for this young negro figuring he'd ran off after killing this captain's wife. When they found the houseboy, he was in the swamp with two bullet holes in the back of his head. It wasn't hard to figure that one out because two months later the camp captain and his redhead got married. The negro couldn't testify that he didn't do it so the man got away with it.

The camps were full of perversion, sodomy, fellatio, and a lot of boys- girls. One of the boy-girls was called Sweet Mama. She worked as a waitress in the little coffee shop up in our dormitory, which was operated by the state. If we had enough money- coffee, sandwiches, and even moonshine whiskey were available to us. Sweet Mama acted just like a girl as she would go around to the different guys taking their orders, and waiting on them. She was the first homosexual I'd ever seen but was no different than the rest of us when it came to work, only when it came to love.

Quite a few men were in Angola for seducing their own daughters. They were Cajuns from the back country of Louisiana. They'd say, "Hell, I raised her, I ought to be able to do what I want with her." Those men couldn't understand why they'd gone to prison.

One man had a farm and three daughters. On the adjoining farm was a man with three sons. The old man and two of his sons raped this farmer's daughters so he went over and killed them. While he was doing life, the other son got into trouble and was sentenced to Angola. As soon as the farmer could get near him, he killed him too, even though the young man had nothing to do with the rape of his daughters.

Another guy tied his grandfather to a peach tree during a thunder storm and raped him. There were men in Angola with crimes that I could hardly believe.

One fellow was serving his third sentence for raping the same woman. We called him "Must Have It". The first time he'd raped her, he was sentenced to ten years. While he was doing that time his brother married the girl. When he got out of prison, he climbed up into a tree and jumped down on her, raping her again. As the story goes, he said, "I must have it." They gave him another ten years and he finished that while I was there. In the meantime, his brother moved to a share-cropping farm. Must

Have It caught his brother's wife out in the field and raped her again. His brother shot him with a shotgun but he lived to come back for another ten years.

Narcotics were no problem to buy inside the prison. Anything you wanted was available for about the same price as on the street. Some of the guys that I worked with, and their friends, had a bad drug habit. At times they would be so sick they couldn't fix themselves so I would take their needle, put "H" in it, and give them a shot. I think that watching their agony was one of the reasons I didn't turn to narcotics to forget where I was at. That and the fact of my father's murder by a dope addict.

Dope would be smuggled in inside of a radio that somebody sent to somebody, or else brought in by the free men. The free men didn't make much money so there were many connections and ways to get drugs into the prison.

The camp barber worked as a connection for dope coming in from New Orleans. One of the nurse's aids was a "backer" for Blacksnake and Jimmy, both dealers. I guess the nurse decided that snitching would get him out of prison but it almost got him killed. One day he was sitting in the barber's chair with a towel wrapped around his neck waiting for a shave. Jimmy and Blacksnake came in with two straight edged razors and proceeded to try to cut the guy's head off. I was standing at the mirror shaving at the time. He struggled out of the chair, dove right out through the window, and lurched over to the fence with blood spilling from his neck. He hit the fence, tried to climb it, and fell to the ground. Some of the guards brought a truck to haul him off to the hospital. I'd never seen a man cut as bad as he was; his voice box was completely destroyed but he lived.

Another man, who was stabbed in the back with a boning knife, walked about twenty steps and dropped dead. Violence was an everyday occurrence and after a while I got used to it.

Mississippi, one of the convict guards, had given the guys a bad time before falling into disfavor with the free men. The camp captain took his khakis away, then threw him back in the yard which was an automatic death sentence. He wasn't in the yard an hour when the guys cornered him just like a pack of dogs after a piece of fresh meat. They beat him, cut him, and literally tore him apart. I think that was the most horrible death a man could ever experience.

Another guard was thrown in the yard but he'd been halfway decent to the guys, so they decided that if he would do fellatio on all of them, he could live. Everybody in the yard lined up and he went from one to the other without stopping; he knew that if he did they would kill him. One guy felt sorry for him and offered him a cup of coffee but he said, "No, I'm hungry, just bring on more meat." From then on his name was Hungry. I felt sorry for him but there was nothing I could do. Certain times during the year we would have to go to the swamps, cut trees down, and carry them up the buggies, and load them. We would wade in that swamp water all day long with those cotton mouthed water moccasins swimming around. Although I don't know why, I can never remember a snake biting anyone. Maybe they just thought they were too good to bite one of us convicts.

Seven days a week, we worked from sun up till sundown without stopping; if anyone shirked, they'd beat him over the head with a club.

For most of us, the only way we could keep going was to chew benzadrine. Benzadrex, an inhalant, came out about then. When the water boy would come around with drinking water, for five cents we could get a cup of coffee. Then we'd tear strips off the inhalant, chew it, and wash it down with coffee. Even though it would burn and blister our mouth, it would give us the push we needed; it kept us going all day long.

It was nothing for a man to maim himself to get out of work. I'd seen men cut off toes, fingers, and even break their legs, anything to get out of the cane fields. One young man, nineteen years old, took a hypodermic needle, filled it with spit, and shot it into his leg. His leg became so infected that they had to cut it off at the knee. The infection kept going and finally the doctor cut it off at the hip. He wouldn't tell the doctors what he had done but they suspected it had been done on purpose. When he got out of the hospital, he couldn't work in the cane field, so they put him driving tractor. To him it was worth losing a leg to get out of that field.

I'd been there a little over a year when my left ankle became infected. It got so bad that I could hardly walk so they finally took me from the cane fields to the hospital.

The doctor decided they'd have to operate on my ankle. He said, "I know you did this on purpose." I wouldn't harm myself in any way as I'd seen too much of it already. My mind was made up that no matter how bad it was, I'd never resort to self-mutilation. Of course, the doctor wasn't convinced.

I was taken into the operating room where two men held me down. They didn't give me anesthetic or anything to deaden the pain while the doctor cut my ankle open, scraped the bone, and put a drain tube in it. I don't think I ever had anything hurt so bad in my life but I made up my mind that I wouldn't scream, so help me God. I wouldn't give them the satisfaction. After the operation, I was taken to a hospital room.

A couple of nurse's aids, Tarzan and Blake, told me they were going to escape out of the hospital and wanted me to go with them. Convict guards were on the towers around the hospital but they'd paid one of the guards fifty dollars to let them go over the fence while he turned his back.

The night we prepared to go; my leg was still bandaged up with the drain tube hanging out. I'd made up my mind I was going even if it meant getting killed in the attempt. I really didn't care.

We hit the fence but the guard had turned us in. They were waiting for us and every one of them started shooting. It sounded like the 4th of July. Tarzan and Blake were shot going over the fence. I got over the fence and took off running but by then they had the horses and dogs after me.

The old captain said I looked like a jackrabbit going off across country. I outran them all the way to the Mississippi River where the dogs finally treed me. So, there I was, up in that tree with those dogs yapping at me.

The old captain came up and pulled out his pistol. He said, "I'm going to kill this Yankee son-of-a-bitch right now." He took a shot at me and hit the tree right by my head. Another man stopped him saying, "No, we'll take him to the RedHat." I knew I was in hell if I went to the RedHat. That was a building comprised entirely of steel with individual cells about the size of a telephone booth. Each cell had a hole in the floor, over the sewer, for a toilet and a faucet sticking out of the wall for drinking water.

They stripped me naked and stuck me in there. Every three days, I was given a meal of beans and rice or grits and gravy. The temperature got up to one-hundred to one-hundred-fifteen degrees in there; it was so hot I could hardly breathe.

During the fifty-eight days that I spent in there, my leg became infected again and they wouldn't give me medical treatment. The red lines were all the way up to my groin. The trustee who took care of the place, smuggled in a bottle of iodine, a razor blade, and a clean T-shirt. I kept cutting it open, pouring iodine in, and bandaging it up. Finally, the infection was cured.

Then my body broke out in boils. I had thirty-two boils on me and no medication. Half the time I was so miserable that I didn't know if I was dead or alive and wished to God that I could die. How I survived, I will never know; I was small but I was tough.

Finally, I got out and went back to the cane fields. They put me in what they called the Red Hat Gang. We wore straw hats painted red, and if we stepped out of line, we'd get shot. We went through hell.

We worked out in the fields on half the rations the others got and had ten minutes to eat them. We were worked seven days a week. When I went out in the morning, I didn't know if I'd be coming in that night or not.

I smuggled a letter out to my folks telling them how unbelievably bad things were for me. Mother wrote back and told me not to talk like that because they might get mad. I couldn't figure out how in the hell they could get any madder than they already were. Mother's letter astonished me.

I don't think any man could survive that place and be completely sane. We had to be a little bit mentally unbalanced by the time we left. I'd built up so much hate that at times it was hard to hold it in. One time, out in the fields, I thought, "God, if only someone would put a machine gun in my hands; I would kill every living thing around me, dogs, cats, convicts, guards, free people, everything that lived, I would destroy."

On two different occasions I was called out of the field and told I was going home. They took me up to the big House, dressed me out, and then told me they'd found out I still had time to do. Back to the Long Line I'd go until finally the day arrived when every day of my time that I owed them was in, and they had to turn me loose.

Six months after I left, the Federal Government stepped in to find out what was going on at that place. Over forty men had cut their heel strings and the newspapers got word of it. Until then, I don't think the government really knew, or even cared about what was happening. All the time I was in Angola not a week went by without a stabbing, murder, or suicide. Even the convict guards, up in the towers, would blow their brains out, and they had it good compared to us. Many a mother's son never got back to his mother. My time in that nightmare was three years and the scars on my body have healed, but the scars inside my mind and heart, I doubt will ever heal because of what happened to me in there.

CHAPTER 8

Going Home But Not For Long

My folks had sent me a train ticket and forty dollars. When I went up to the Big House, they dressed me up in khakis. It was twenty-seven miles to the nearest town, up a dirt road, and out of the swamps. I was told, "Get there the best way you know how."

A colored kid was getting out that same day and his father was coming to get him. They gave me a ride to St. Francisville and I caught the bus from there to Baton Rouge. The colored kid got on the bus with me, so I said to him, "When we get to Baton Rouge, we are going to hit the Honky Tonks and really have fun." He said, "I can't go with you. They don't allow me in them places for white folks." I said, "To hell with them, you're going with me anyway."

Well, some way or another, he got off the bus without me seeing him. The poor devil was scared to death because he knew I would get him killed.

My train didn't leave until the next day so that night I went out to a roadhouse for a few drinks and a decent meal. I bit into a piece of white bread and I guess I was so starved for sugar that it tasted just like cake.

I started talking to a salesman from New Orleans. He told me all about what he sold and then said, "I have a brother in Baton Rouge who's the overseer out at Angola."

I went berserk. The poor guy didn't have anything to do with Angola but I just flipped my wig. I busted him alongside the head with a beer bottle and cut him up pretty bad, but I got out of there without being busted.

The next morning, I was on the train leaving Louisiana, heading for Montana. To this day I have never been back to Louisiana and would never go back unless they carried me- then I'd have to be dead.

It was evening when I arrived at my folks. They didn't know when I was coming home so I took a taxi to their house. My stepfather came to the door when I knocked. He said, "Yes, is there something I can do for you?" He didn't even know who I was, so I said, "It's Grant, can I come in?" I heard my mother say, "On my God, it'd my son!" She threw her arms around me. I'd changed so much in those three years that they hadn't recognized me.

We put men in those places, try to control their minds, and do nothing for them. Prison makes them worse, then turns them loose on society again. There is no such thing as rehabilitation; there could be, but what the answer is, I don't know. We still don't have it in this day and age.

Louisiana has a new penitentiary now, new buildings, everything is new but they still have the same old punishment. Whether they have convict guards or not, I don't know. I ran into a man recently who'd done time down there in '73, and he said they did. Maybe they have less brutality and a little better food but it's still a chain gang without chains. They have the sugar cane fields, the vegetable gardens, and they still work with mules.

Maybe they have a few more tractors now but it's such a waste of mankind.

In the South, many other places aren't any better; places like Huntsville in Texas and Parchment in Mississippi. They still work them out in the fields and treat them like dogs.

I knew I couldn't adapt to society again. Nightmares were frequent, I was restless, and couldn't stand authority of any kind. When someone told me to do something, I automatically rebelled. I couldn't hold a job; I'd had numerous jobs but couldn't stay in one place.

My folks had moved to Red Lodge and opened up Budd's Fixit Shop.

For a while I worked around the shop then went to work in the cannery.

Nobody knew of the trouble I'd been in. One night I got drunk and ran out of money so I wrote some bad checks and signed my name to them.

The Red Lodge police arrested me and that was the first time I'd ever been inside of our county jail. It had hammocks to sleep on and an old stove for cooking our meals.

Budd made arrangements to get me out of jail but they'd found out about my time in Angola so they had no choice but to try me for the bad checks. I received two years in the Montana State Prison in DeerLodge.

I'll never forget the day I arrived there; when they were bringing me in as a "fish", they were carrying a guy out on a stretcher with a pair of scissors stuck in his stomach. I thought, "My God, what have I got myself into now, from one hell to another."

After I'd been there for a while, I realized it wasn't quite as bad as Angola, but DeerLodge was all cell time. They locked me up the day I arrived and I stayed in that cell, except for a shower once a week, until the day I left.

Forks and knives were not allowed so I ate my meals out of a bowl with a spoon.

The only jobs were working in the mess hall or the Tag Plant, making license plates. I learned to do leather work, made myself a few dollars, and kept busy. The two years were rather uneventful; I finished my time and got out.

A roofing and siding job was waiting for me, one that I'd applied for while I was in prison. I worked in Montana and Wyoming for about seven months. I was drinking fairly heavy all the time. One night, I started drinking in Story, Wyoming. The next thing I knew, I was in jail in Buffalo. I'd gone to Buffalo, ran out of money so wrote some bad checks. One was to a motel so I'd probably met a girl. The judge sentenced me to two years in Rawlins, the Wyoming State Prison.

While I was there, I went into leather work again; by then I was pretty good at it. After I'd been there for seven months, they decided to make me a trustee. They gave me outside work and I decided I was going to leave. I could see no reason why I should stay, so one morning when I went to work, I hopped a freight train loaded with oranges and hid.

The train carried me all the way out of Wyoming. For two days and nights all I ate were oranges, which was the best physic I ever had. I got off the train up in Idaho, broke, with no place to stay. I ran into a woman I'd known years before when she was running a house of prostitution in Idaho. I stayed with her for two months, then left and knocked around the country for a while.

Finally, I got busted up in Yakima, Washington. They found out I was an escapee; the Wyoming authorities were called and the prison warden came after me. He took me back to Rawlins where I was promptly put in the "hole." Their hole, at that time, was on Death Row. I sat in my cell and all day long looked at the Gas Chamber. One meal was served every three days.

As I said, I rebelled against any authority so when I was doing time in DeerLodge, I spent half of that in the hole. When a guard would tell me to do something, I would tell him what he could do with it; I was the same at Rawlins.

I spent five months in the hole and probably would have gotten out sooner, but I wouldn't cooperate. Eventually they let me out and I went back to my leather work. My time finally came to an end.

When I went home, I opened a leather shop in back of my folks' store, in RedLodge. My stepdad financed me and I paid him back as my business progressed. My business became good enough that I had a salesman out selling leather goods while I took care of the store.

CHAPTER 9

Dorothy

Every once in a while, I like to look back at the happiness I've had. The best years of my life were spent with Dorothy. She'd come to RedLodge on vacation but ran out of money, so she went to work in a local cafe waiting tables. I was attracted to Dorothy Wolfe instantly and asked her to go out with me.

She was a doll; petite in build with an impish smile, sparkling blue eyes, and short, silver-grey hair. Dorothy was always outgoing and the life of the party no matter where we went. It was a joy to go out with her because she seemed to bring people around with her vivacious personality. Dorothy was a beautiful dancer; something I liked to do very much.

The time flew by that May. By the month's end, she'd earned enough money to get back to Santa Rosa, California, her home. After that we called each other frequently. I just couldn't get her off my mind; sleep was impossible and my days were almost as lonely as my evenings.

My mother left for Salt Lake to visit an aunt right after Dorothy's departure so one morning at three, I woke Budd up and told him I was leaving for California. He asked, "When?" and I said, "Right now." Budd loaned me two-hundred dollars for the trip and I got in my car and left.

My car broke down in Twin Falls, Idaho so I parked it there and took the bus to Santa Rosa. Nearly thirty years have gone by since that June day when I hailed a cab from the bus depot out to Dorothy's house. She was the essence of my life but I didn't realize it until many years later.

Soon after my arrival, Dorothy packed her suitcase and we took the bus back to Idaho and my car. After it was fixed, we drove to Nevada where we were married.

Our marriage was a surprise to my folks. They'd about given up on me by then because I was already thirty-one years old. My stepdad gave us a big roll of bills, all ones; I don't think I'd ever seen so many dollar bills in my life.

Dorothy and I rented a little apartment in RedLodge. She got a job in a cafe and I went back to work in my leather shop. Dorothy was one hell of a waitress; she could make more money in tips than most people made in wages.

Two months after we were married, a friend of mine from Cody, Wyoming, came to see me about some leather goods for his store. He liked my work and wanted me to go into a partnership with him. Dorothy thought it was a good opportunity for me, so we moved to Cody.

The Cody Saddle Company's downtown location attracted tourists and was convenient for area ranchers. Harry took care of the store while I fashioned various leather goods. Two salesmen worked for us selling to individuals and other stores.

Most of my free time was spent drinking; all I wanted to do was forget the past and make up for all those years I'd lost in prison. Several months after we'd moved to Cody, I decided to sell my share of the business back to Harry and travel for a while.

Dorothy and I decided to visit her daughter in Kentucky. Her husband was stationed at Fort Campbell. I bought a car at Tracey Motors, there in Cody, and financed it, before we left; they gave us permission to take it to Kentucky.

We left Cody with a few of my leather goods and several thousand dollars. While we were at Fort Campbell, I took a ham up to some colored people so they could barbecue it. The old guy was sitting on the front porch in his rocking chair when he saw my Wyoming license plates. He wanted to hear all about the cowboys and Indians we had back in Wyoming. They asked me if I was a drinking man and I told them that I'd been known to drink one or two. He said, "Well, I have got some white lightning." I got the ham barbecued and myself too. That was the first time my wife got mad at me. She liked to drink and enjoy herself but she had a better head on her shoulders than I did.

Dorothy wanted to go from her daughter's back to California. We drove to Santa Rosa, where her sister was, and stayed with her for a while. I went to work in a plywood mill, but after a few weeks we left and went to Smith River, California where I went to work at the 'Ship N Shore". Dorothy worked there as a cocktail waitress. We were there for about six months when the State Police came and arrested me for taking mortgaged property out of Wyoming. I tried to explain to them that I'd been making payments but they carted me off to jail in Crescent City. What had happened was, I had been late on the first payment so Tracey Motors had sworn out a warrant for my arrest. When they'd received that payment along with the second one, the warrant was canceled but the teletype still had me listed as wanted. Well, I got that straightened out and later received a letter of apology from the finance company.

My car was paid for by then but I'd lost my job when my record came to be known. Dorothy was still working but we were both restless; we were never satisfied with our jobs or where we were at.

We traveled for a year all over the country after we left Crescent City. If we couldn't find work, I always had a way of coming up with some cash. Dorothy knew I was a thief and hustler. She wouldn't take a nickel that didn't belong to her but she never condemned me for anything.

We ran short of cash so I burglarized a jewelry store and filled the trunk with several thousand dollars' worth of jewelry. The silent alarm must have gone off because a roadblock was already up by the time, I picked Dorothy and our little chihuahua up at the hotel. I didn't dare turn around or go around it; that would have looked suspicious. They were stopping all the cars and searching them. When they got to us, the patrolman looked into the car from my wife's side. Our little dog was on her lap barking furiously at him. I leaned towards Dorothy and asked, "Officer, what seems to be the trouble?" He told me about the jewelry store.

I said, "I can't understand who'd do a thing like that. They should be in prison." The dog was licking his hand by then.

"Well," he said, "you folks can go on. I can tell by looking at you that you wouldn't have anything to do with it."

Dorothy's eyes were on me all the way through that roadblock. I didn't have to say anything; she knew darn well I'd done it even before I told her.

I lay pretty low for a while after that. The jewelry haul was enough to last until summer with the jobs we picked up here and there.

We stopped in a small California town on the 4th of July broke, and needing a job before we could go on. Dorothy went to work in a restaurant while I cruised around town looking for a bar tending job. When I walked into one bar, I spotted this woman paying for some drinks with a roll of twenties. Right then, I forgot about asking for a job and proceeded to figure out how to steal that roll of money.

She was sitting on a bar stool with one big lumberjack on her left and another one on her right. I only had a couple of dollars in my pocket but I sat down beside the guy on her left and ordered a drink. The twenties were in a small purse inside of her handbag which made it all the better for me. With the place full of people celebrating the 4th, the bartender was too busy to watch what I was doing. I reached under her logger friend's arm and into the handbag swiftly removing the small purse. They never knew that I had it. After I finished my drink, I left for a while.

When I came back a couple of hours later, the bar was damn near empty and torn up. The bartender proceeded to tell me what had happened, "This lady reached into her purse to pay me for some drinks and her money was gone. One big lumberjack accused another one of taking it, then they started yelling accusations at each other like a couple of idiots. Before I could quiet them down, they were in a fist fight. The lady's screaming about her money and every damn customer in this place is swinging at somebody. By the time the police got here, my business was already wrecked."

I bought him a couple of drinks and he returned the favor. I tried to listen with great sympathy all the time wishing that I'd stayed to watch the excitement.

We traveled throughout California for several months working wherever I or Dorothy could find a job. I'd been out of prison for almost three years by then.

My folks asked us to come home for the holidays so we left for Red Lodge. Winter snows were already falling in the mountains by the time we arrived. Neither of us were used to the cold weather so right after New Year's, we decided to go back to California.

I drove on ice slicked roads all the way from Red Lodge to Missoula the first day. We checked into a motel there and that night Dorothy got sick, and I had to take her to the hospital. I was frantic; we didn't have enough money to pay the motel bill for several nights let alone a hospital bill and I wasn't about to ask my folks for any more money.

One way or another I was going to get the money we needed. I'd acquired a pistol from a friend; this was the first time I'd had a gun in my possession. Before, I would never touch one for fear of what I might do with it. Hate and bitterness were always seething inside even though I acted cheerful around Dorothy and my folks.

That night, I started out to rob a grocery store but my car slid on the ice and ended up in a snow drift. A citizen called the police to help me out of my predicament. They sure did; in the process they found the gun in the glove compartment of the car. This friend had said the gun wasn't "hot" and I'd believed him. When the police ran a check on it, they found out it had been used in the burglary of a Billings saddle shop. I couldn't tell the police who he was or how I got the gun so they took me to jail.

My folks came up to Missoula and hired a lawyer named Goldman. He suggested that with my past record the best thing I could do was plead guilty. The judge sentenced me to six years in the Montana State Prison. Within seventeen days, I was back behind those prison bars.

Dorothy had a tumor removed from her uterus confining her to the hospital for several weeks. Right after that she moved to DeerLodge and went to work at the 4-B's Cafe which was across the street from the prison.

It was so hard; me being in that place with her out there. After a few weeks, I asked the warden to move me to a different cell. I just couldn't stand to look out my cell window and see her every day. She paid her hospital bill and put enough money on the books so I could do leather work but my heart wasn't in my work, so most of the time I sat and stared at the bars surrounding my cell. Dorothy would come visit me on Sundays and each time, it was harder to see her leave.

I'd been in there three years when I was promoted to Trustee. When that happened, I made arrangements to meet my wife because I was going to escape. I was working in the Block Plant making cinder blocks and had access to a vehicle. The first time my supervisor left me alone, I jumped into one of the trucks to leave.

A friend came running and asked, "Where are you going?" I said, "I'm leaving."

He replied, "Then there's no sense in me sticking around here. I'll go with you."

We drove the truck as far as we dared then hid it. From there we went on foot into the mountains. A search party with guns, dogs, and high-powered lights was on our trail. They hunted for us that night and almost caught us twice. It was stop breathing or be caught; they were that close. My stomach was in knots, chills were running all over my body, and the hair on my arms seemed electrified. I was just that scared.

Johnny and I moved from the mountains down to the flat land that night. The snow was several feet deep in places. There was absolutely no way we'd make it over those mountains to Phillipsburg without freezing our feet.

The darkness wouldn't hide us for very long so I told Johnny, "We'd better try to hide in a haystack until dark then try to make it to a phone tonight. I can call my wife and let her know where we are then."

Whoever owned the farm was feeding his cattle from the stack because the hay was loose and dry. We burrowed deep into the top of that stack and fell asleep instantly. When the cattle wouldn't come near the haystack the farmer became suspicious and called his neighbors. I awoke with a start to see twenty men, armed with rifles and shotguns, around us. A couple of them started punching us with their guns, telling us to move out or they'd shoot to kill.

We were taken back to prison and thrown in the "hole". The hole was down under the cellblock where the prison's boiler system was located. It would get so hot from those steam pipes that I could hardly breathe. The guards handcuffed me to one of the doors in a position that prohibited me from standing up or sitting down. I was kept that way for seven days and nights. With the effects from the steam pipes, leg cramps, and a constant backache, I almost fainted many times.

When they finally took me out of the hole, I couldn't even stand up straight. Because of the escape attempt, my head was shaved and they put me in stripes for six months.

After those six months were up, things became fairly normal. Dorothy could come see me again on Sundays but for six months our visits were restricted to telephone conversations with me confined to a wire cage, and heavy glass between us.

I was given eighteen months more for the escape, and had that plus three years of my sentence left when Montana instituted their first parole board. When I went before the board, they reduced the time to the eighteen months.

Dorothy was getting restless; she wanted to move but she didn't want to be away from me. The loneliness was worse for her than it was for me because she was denied a real marriage, but she wouldn't go out on me. She stayed in DeerLodge for the rest of that year then left for California. I was supposed to meet her there when I was paroled.

CHAPTER 10

DeerLodge Riot

Unfortunately, I was still in DeerLodge when the '59 riot occurred. It is really hard to describe what went on during the five days of convict control. Lots of psychos are kept in prisons. When the riot started, they were running around with knives and clubs trying to start something, while at the same time afraid to, for fear they couldn't finish it.

Jerry Myles, the convict who started the riot, had done time in California, Kansas, Illinois, Texas, and Georgia. The younger convicts, who didn't know any better, followed Myles. They thought he would help them escape but all he had in mind was a personal vendetta for deputy Warden Theodore Rothe. Both Myles and Smart, homosexual lovers, were psychotic as hell.

Myles had been a convict boss when Rothe came to work at the prison and was permitted to work unsupervised in the prison garment shop where he took full advantage of his power by sexually using the younger inmates. When Rothe and his administration cracked down, by eliminating all the convict guards, Myles decided to get even. For a while he was able to continue his homosexual activities and he tried to regain the power he was losing while all the time plotting revenge.

Warden Powell wasn't in favor of allowing the guards to carry rifles for fear an inmate would gain control of one. However, the guards were afraid to be without them so he conceded.

Six-gun towers rose above the massive rock walls surrounding the prison; the walls served as walkways between each of the towers. On April 16, 1959, Myles, Smart, and a small group of convicts cornered a lone guard up on the walkway; they doused him with cleaning fluid they'd stolen from the garment shop then they approached him with lighted torches. The guard gave up his rifle without a struggle.

Myles and his followers went from there into the cellblock where they disarmed another guard. After locking him up, they headed to the prison kitchen where they overpowered those guards and locked them up. Armed with knives from the kitchen and several rifles, they continued their course. Twenty-three guards were locked up and still no one was aware that the convicts had control.

After overpowering the guard at the gate, Myles, Smart, and a third convict casually walked into the administration building. Myles was after Rothe; he burst in the deputy warden's door yelling, "I'm going to kill you!" As Myles went after Rothe with a knife, Cox, the guard who was with Rothe, tried to defend him but was slashed in the arm. Lee Smart raised his rifle and shot Rothe through the heart. Myles had his revenge.

Carefully working their way through the administration building and the other cellblock, the three convicts took all of the guards who were on duty and locked them up. The inside of the prison was now under their control. Myles wasn't too concerned about the few remaining wall guards; he already had twenty-three guards locked up as hostages.

One of the guards was forced to call Warden Powell whose office was across the street from the prison. Powell entered the prison and was taken hostage. Myles forced Powell into calling the governor, demanding that he and his followers be allowed to walk out of the prison unharmed, or else all of the hostages would die.

But the inmate Myles left guarding the warden, suddenly changed his mind. "I can't kill anybody," he said. While Myles and his partners were still occupied in another part of the prison, Powell and his convict friend left the administration building. Powell notified the wall guard that he was coming out through the main gate and the inmate would be with him. Of the 425 inmates in the prison, only 20 had followed Myles.

With his only chance of escape thwarted, Myles decided to try bargaining for better prison conditions. There wasn't any doubt about the need for better conditions but I've never seen anything change for the better through violence.

The hospital's medicine cabinet was broken into so narcotics were available to anyone who wanted them. Some of the convicts brought out their "Pruno", an alcoholic drink frequently concocted by prisoners having access to the kitchen pantry. Nearly everyone was drunk or high on pills and homosexual activities were abundant.

Like a lot of things that start, there wasn't any control; nobody could decide on what specific conditions they wanted changed. First, they'd have one list of demands, then another. The warden promised nothing so everything came to a standstill. The press came and we conversed with them through a loudspeaker. We asked for recreation, better food, and more rights. All we had was cell time then except for a shower once a week, and our daily trips to the mess hall. We ate beans, using a spoon and bowl, then returned directly to our cells. For the smallest violation, we'd be sent to the hole where we were handcuffed to the bars and subjected to intense heat from the steam pipes. Rothe wanted to change all that when he came to the prison but he never had a chance.

The Montana governor, at that time, we called The Galloping Swede. He had no use for any of the prisoners and if it had been up to him, he'd have sent a squad in immediately to take control of the prison. Various sheriff 's units and the State Police were sent to surround the place. Deer Lodge citizens armed themselves because they feared a massive prison break. They didn't realize that there wasn't any way we could reach the walls without being shot down.

We heard, on a prison radio, that the National Guard was coming in the next day. Everybody was uptight, not knowing what to expect from the Guard. Jerry Myles and his sidekick went up into one of the towers so they could open fire in case the National Guard stormed the cell house. Nobody slept and we all milled around. We didn't know what to do; what good would a club or anything else do against soldiers with guns. Most of us didn't want any more killing. Rothe's death had been enough.

Some of the convicts threatened to burn the guards who were locked up if the prison was stormed. They'd stocked up on flammable naphtha and rags just in case. The hostages covered their cell doors with mattresses hoping to protect themselves against being burned alive. Due to some level heads, convicts armed with knives, were trying to protect the guards, especially those who had treated some of the guys ill during their years of incarceration. Believe me, there were some sadistic guards whose lives wouldn't have been worth much if the inmates they'd harmed had gotten to them.

Several fires were set; one in the kitchen which we promptly put out; then another to the offices inside the administration building. We put that one out then had to run over to the theatre and stop a fire there. The theatre was donated by a man named Clark, the founder of the Anaconda Copper Mining Company. It was a nice building and our only source of entertainment; we sure didn't want it burned.

I was head cook so I tried to keep food out for the guys. We had no idea how much longer the riot would last. Our families and friends were watching from the outside not knowing what was going on inside the walls.

Dorothy was still working right across the street at the 4-B's; once in a while I would catch a glimpse of her as she paced back and forth wondering how I was.

Somehow the National Guard found out where the two-armed convicts were and what tier the guards were locked up on. Before they stormed the penitentiary, a bazooka team was sent up into one of the towers to try to knock Myles and Smart out. They put two rounds of explosives through Myles' tower but failed to hit either of the convicts. At the same time, the Guard came in through a small door in the wall by the abandoned women's quarters. (Montana sent their female prisoners to other states for incarceration.) The armed convicts fired from their position striking one of the Guard's lieutenants.

The National Guardsmen stormed the cellblock, blowing the door open to gain entry. As they came in, they threw lead in every direction, off the walls, cells, and galleries keeping everyone away from Number Five Tier where the guards were locked up. They rounded all of us up and ran us out into the yard for strip-shake. In the meantime, Lee Smart shot Jerry Myles then turned his gun on himself. At 19, he'd committed his third and last murder.

After we were stripped and searched, the guard went through all the cells throwing everything over the tiers; all of our hobbies, tools, and personal affects, everything we worked with. As soon as they were finished, we were ran back in naked and locked up.

We had complete control of the prison for five days but at the end of those five days, there was hell to pay! They kept us locked up for two months, feeding nothing but sandwiches and coffee, twice a day. Everybody stanks to high heaven because we never got out to shower. If we thought conditions were bad before the riot, they were a hell of a lot worse afterwards.

The State Police took over the guard duty and we had nothing but harassment from them all the time they were there. There was some brutality; they'd take some of the convicts out of their cells, question them, work them over, then throw them back in.

I was released a few months after the riot. Instead of going to my wife, I started drinking and running around the country. I was a pretty selfish person then; it is sad that I had to pass a certain point in life before realizing how precious it really is. We only have one go around at life and so much can be done with it and should be, then I destroyed so much of mine without ever realizing its value.

CHAPTER 11

Atlanta

The ski run near RedLodge was being built when I paroled out of DeerLodge. I went to work on that and stayed with my parents.

One morning, when I was getting ready to go to work, my grandmother came over and told me to take Mother to the hospital. Grandma wouldn't tell me what was wrong but I soon found out. My stepfather had a heart attack that morning; instead of alarming my mother, the hospital notified Grandma. By the time we got to the hospital Budd was dead.

I don't think I'd ever realized how much I really loved Budd until that morning. After I took his clothes out to the car, I sat there by myself and cried like a baby. One of the nurses came out to get me because Mother collapsed, so I had to snap out of it and take her home.

Right after the funeral, I ended up in Livingston, Montana on a running drunk. It seemed like every time something was bothering me, I'd just go get drunk.

Someone left the keys in their car so I took off in it. The authorities caught me down in the state of Georgia. I had committed a federal offense by taking a stolen car across state lines so the judge sentenced me to three years in Atlanta, which is a maximum-security federal penitentiary.

I'd been out of Deer Lodge less than six months when I was picked up for that. Prisons are regimented a lot like the military; you get up, eat, work, and go to bed at a certain time. I could function okay inside those prison walls but I just couldn't seem to muster the stability it takes to perform out in society.

Atlanta Federal Penitentiary is located right outside of Atlanta, Georgia. My first job there was in the stubble room of the cotton mill but the cotton was so thick I couldn't stand it. After that, they put me to work running an elevator which was an easy job and one that I liked.

While I was in Atlanta, I met some of the Mafia family. The famous Valachi, who told all to the government, and Genovese. I guess Valachi didn't have much choice, the Mafia was going to have him killed, so he turned informer to save his life.

Genovese would go for walks out in the prison yard with his bodyguard. His bodyguard had the coldest blue eyes I'd ever seen; they were completely dead and when I looked into them all I could see was death.

They had a guy in Atlanta called the Sniper who was from Washington D.C. Whatever happened in his life to turn him against colored people, I don't know, but he would pop out of manholes or doorways and shoot negroes. He got quite a few of them before he was caught.

The Sniper loved baseball and played on the prison's ball team. We couldn't get a colored man within twenty yards of him, even during a baseball game; they were scared to death of him. He was really a hell of a nice guy but he just didn't like colored people.

One of my favorite sports was go-cart racing. We'd set up the track out in the prison yard and kids from the outside would bring their go-carts. The cons would bet on the go-cart racers. They would get excited, step out in front of those kids, and get run over. Convicts would get carried off to the hospital with broken legs but it was all part of the game. Those kids could really drive those go-carts; they would go like a bat out of hell. One little shaver could hardly see over the steering wheel but he was my favorite. I'd bet on him every time.

I also worked in the kitchen while I was there. In the basement part, they had these big barrels; they'd hold about 500 gallons. When they peeled spuds, they put them in those barrels. I'll never forget the day I went down to get something and looked over in one of them barrels. All I could see was a black ass sticking out. Somebody had killed a negro and stuffed him in with the spuds. I guess he'd been fooling around with someone's "kid" or something, and someone got him.

That was one thing that was taboo in most prisons. Some of the guys had their own "girlfriends". I call them girlfriends but it was usually some young kid who wanted somebody to take care of him. He'd have himself a "daddy" and become that daddy's exclusive property. Believe me, nobody fooled with Daddy's kid; in fact, no one even spoke to him. We stayed completely away from him because his daddy was extremely jealous, just like a man would be over his own girlfriend.

The colored men had their own separate cell houses until the Civil Rights Movement started, then they decided to integrate. They were going to stick one negro in every eight-man cell. Well, they tried it with three negroes and all they did was get them killed, so they decided right then that there would be no forced integration. Out in the free world, integration wasn't stopped that way but it sure was in there.

I was still raising hell and, on the prod, so after eighteen months, they transferred me to Leavenworth. Leavenworth is also a maximum-security federal pen which is located about thirty-five miles from Kansas City, Kansas.

Atlanta hadn't been a bad place to do time but prison life is so completely different from life out in society. It's a world in itself with its own rules and regulations, sort of a home code that we have to live by. In a way it's a jungle just like it's a jungle on the outside. But as long as we do our own time, mind our own business, and keep our word, we can do our time without any trouble from the other convicts.

Some people are very fortunate; they learn early, by their mistakes, and go on to a productive life. Some of us "hardheads" have to waste many years behind bars before we finally wake up to the realization that we are throwing our life away, and wasting our most productive years when we could accomplish so much and be a benefit to society and not a detriment. When I was young jail didn't mean much to me. I'd lost my fear of them and once that fear is gone, it is very easy to get back in.

I was one of the unfortunate ones because when I was young, life was all a lark. What I didn't realize was that I was slowly growing older and I was doing it in a penitentiary. Life was passing me by. I was missing so many of the good things, a family, children, and even a job; a steady job. What a waste of life.

One thing about the federal penitentiaries, we had a chance to improve ourselves. Convicts could learn a trade, go to college, or further their education. I never had anything like that in mind. I guess I didn't care one way or another about life then. I never tried to stay out, didn't give a damn about society, and was pretty much a rebel.

CHAPTER 12

Leavenworth

I was in Leavenworth twice. When I was transferred from Atlanta in '61, I spent eight months and eleven days in there. My second stay began May 1, 1970 and ended with my transfer to the McNeil Island Federal Penitentiary, April 23, 1972.

Leavenworth holds about three thousand men. It is built like a wagon wheel; the hub is the control center and the spokes are the cell houses.

My jobs were in the kitchen and shoe factory while I was in Leavenworth. They put me up on second floor, running a sewing machine, sewing counters for shoes. That paid fifty cents an hour so I was able to make about a hundred dollars a month. Federal prisons pay better than those run by the states. I never made much more than fifty cents a day at any job in a state institution. I could at least save money towards my release in Federal penitentiaries.

I shared an eight-man cell with seven other men. One was a bootlegger, one was an artist, and five were Hells Angels, the motorcycle riders. The Hells Angels were really characters; they told me tales of their escapades and scores I wouldn't dare repeat. They were all in there for using or dealing narcotics.

The old bootlegger was from Kentucky. This was his third time in prison for running moonshine. He would stay about a year, then contact the judge; the judge would cut the rest of his time, let him out, and he'd be right back to running moonshine again. The government figured he owed them at least a quarter of a million in taxes off that booze, but they never could collect anything.

The artist was from Alcatraz. When they began closing "The Rock", convicts were shipped from there to various institutions. After seeing his work, I asked him to teach me how to paint. Although I became pretty good at it, I could never really improve on my work. I sold a few paintings but finally gave up because I felt I would never be a good painter.

I met Frank Costello in Leavenworth. He was a "don" of the Mafia, the head of one of the Mafia families. Frank was kind of a gravel-voiced character, a nice guy and very polite, but I knew if he was crossed, he would dispose of that person in a minute. He was one of my regular customers when I worked in the kitchen. I used to sell him steaks, sandwiches, and coffee. There was nothing unusual about him except when I saw him on the yard; he always had a bodyguard.

There were some Puerto Ricans there. Remember the ones that shot up the Senate? They were very patriotic, very zealous, and rather funny. I couldn't help but like them. I had to laugh every time I thought of them shooting up the Senate.

I met Randolph Abel, the famous spy, the United States traded for U-2 pilot Gary Powers. He looked like a big farmer but he was a very intelligent man, rather shy, and pretty much of a loner.

Many things happened while I was there. One guard was killed up on my tier. Three Mexicans caught him in the back of the tier, cut him up, and robbed him of his watch and what money he had. They wanted dope and he had the money. Usually a guard never walked alone; they were always in pairs. This one made the mistake of being by himself.

When someone would "snitch", other convicts would burn his cell with him in it. Because of their various jobs, convicts had access to flammable liquids; ether was used in the hospital so it was easy for a convict nurse or patient to steal that; those who worked in the garage or laundry could get hold of gas or naphtha. Usually, the guard who was doing the shake-down would find it but sometimes the unsuspecting guard would miss it. Once the convict made it through body search, he was free to go on to his cell with whatever he had. He would fashion a Molotov cocktail by filling a bottle with the flammable liquid, stick a rag in the top for a wick, and it was ready for use. All he'd have to do was walk by the "snitch's" cell, light the rag, and throw it in. He had to move fast or it would get him too.

If a convict wants to live, snitching is the worst thing he can do. He may think he will get out of prison sooner or gain the guards' favor, but all he's doing is setting himself up to be killed.

Down in the rotunda that we'd walk through to go to our meals, they had one of those mechanical Santa's on a pedestal. He would wave his hands, bow, and holler, "Ho, ho, ho, Merry Christmas!" They put that up about two weeks before Christmas and every time we would go to chow, we'd have to pass that damned thing and listen to it.

One morning, just before Christmas, we were going single file to chow, and old Santa was hollering, "Ho, ho, ho, Merry Christmas." One guy ran out of line and kicked him dead in the ass. He yelled, "Ho, ho, ho, Merry Christmas, you son-of-a-bitch!" Everybody laughed. Naturally they hauled the guy off to the hole. Well, he kicked old Santa hard enough to put him out of commission for that year, so we didn't have to worry about him anymore.

The guard, in the control room, called me from my tier one day. I was taken up to the front of the place where the Sheriff was waiting to hand me divorce papers. Dorothy and I had been apart seven years by then. She'd finally gotten tired of waiting and decided to divorce me, which I could understand. She was too good a woman for me.

I was notified by phone when my grandmother passed away. Nothing has ever hurt me more in my life than that. I went back to my cell and cried and cried; not so much over losing her because I knew she was old, but that I couldn't be there. Of all the people who'd cared about me, I'd loved her the most and felt the worst whenever I'd let her down. My life had to have been a vast disappointment to her.

A lot of well-known entertainers would come to Leavenworth. That was always a bright spot in my prison time. If they were playing in Kansas City, they'd take time out to come out and perform for us. Johnny Cash and June Carter were there. They set up their stage in the big yard.

Everyone was out there, say three thousand men. Johnny and June put on a good performance then afterwards, before the guards could stop them, they got down off the stage and began mingling with the men. Of course, the guards were scared to death of what would happen to them. They didn't realize that the men loved these performers and there was no way in hell they would ever get hurt.

When Tiny Tim performed for us, he played in the inside theater. He came out on stage in his tennis shoes, with a little mandolin, singing, "Tip Toe Through the Tulips". It was so disgusting that we booed him out of the theater. Everyone got up and walked out. He was the only performer that came out to Leavenworth that nobody would stay and listen to.

Leavenworth was one of many prisons stops along the way for me. I didn't realize it then, but the frequency of incarceration was probably the only thing that kept the alcohol or my antics from killing me.

CHAPTER 13

McNeil Island

I was in McNeil three different times. After leaving Leavenworth, my parole was revoked because I'd robbed a store and I had to spend two-hundred and ninety days in McNeil. My sentence began August 23, 1962, and ended March 8, 1963.

They raised a lot of fruit on the island. I worked in the cannery the first time I was there. We canned apples, plums, cherries, and peaches for various Federal institutions.

McNeil sits out on an island off Puget Sound. Puget Sound is a body of water in the state of Washington. McNeil is something like Alcatraz, but it isn't a maximum-security prison.

August 4, 1964, I began my second stay at McNeil. I decided to learn a trade while I was in that time so I went to work in the upholstery shop. We had a teacher who really knew his business. I worked for him a little over two years and during that time learned an awful lot.

I have always loved to work with my hands so after I learned the upholstery trade, I took a barber course and passed it with flying colors. The course they taught was accredited, so I received a diploma and no one would ever know that I'd learned the barber trade in a penitentiary. My second stay ended December 5, 1967. I managed to stay out of prisons for a bit over three years that time.

My third and last time in McNeil began April 23, 1972 when I was transferred from Leavenworth. I'd worked in Little Rock, Arkansas and

Viet Nam prior to that run in with the law which netted me another three years. I started my time in Leavenworth and finished it in McNeil.

I had a lot of freedom on McNeil Island. In the summertime, I used to sit out in the yard and play chess with a friend. The man had a lot of problems; alcohol was one and his wife was another. She was always giving him a bad time over their little twin boys. He'd had a nervous breakdown so the doctors kept him on pills or tranquilizers all the time he was in McNeil.

When he had his time in and got back out on the streets, he went back to drinking. One morning after he'd left, I was listening to the radio and on the news, I heard his name mentioned. I listened more closely and found out he'd hung himself. He was drinking when he checked into a motel, then about three in the morning, he left with their television set. The owner saw him and called the police. They put him in jail and an hour later, when they went to check his cell, he'd hung himself. Such a waste.

I've run into so many different kinds of people in these places. I knew the Barker brothers of the notorious twenties and Frank Beck, the Teamster boss, who got busted for misusing union funds.

They had an old wino in McNeil who had a picture of a wine bottle pinned up on his wall. All his life, he'd wanted to get all the winos on Skid Road drunk so he got off a freight train in Sacramento, went in and robbed a bank. He ran down to Skid Row with about seventeen hundred dollars and sat there, in a bar, passing out five-dollar bills to all the winos. Well, by the time the police found him all the winos were drunk, he was happy, and the money was gone. He'd finally accomplished his lifelong ambition but they gave him fifteen years for it too.

This wino worked with me putting glass in the windows of the powerhouse. The powerhouse faced the baseball field and ball players were always breaking the glass. A lot of the windows were odd shaped so the glass had to be precisely cut to fit. I worked for about two months putting in windows and couldn't understand why it was taking so long. One day I caught him; when I'd put the window in, he'd crack or break it. He said he liked the job so well that he just didn't want it to end. He was quite a character, that guy.

I've seen so much of life in these places; the good and the bad. There are as many drugs and almost as much booze as there is out in the free world, and not a hell of a lot more expensive either. It seems that booze and drugs are two of the devil's greatest play things.

McNeil had a furniture factory where they would strip down furniture and refinish it. The vat that they dipped furniture in had this tetraethyl chloride in it. Convicts would put that on rags and sniff it; it would make them high. There were five Indians who sniffed that stuff all the time. It killed two of them and two more ended up as vegetables. Their minds were completely gone. The other one had to be shipped to Springfield, Missouri because he had little mind left. (They have a large federal prison hospital in Springfield.) It seems a man will do anything to get high in these places so he can forget where he is at. But if he hates it so much, why does he keep coming back?

Two boys, from Canada, who spoke French but not English were in McNeil. One of them ran off, but out there on that island, it's seven miles of water to the mainland and freedom. So, he was still on the island and they were hunting for him. The guys were kidding his brother; telling him what they would do with him after he was caught. They scared the guy so bad that he killed himself.

He lived up in the top tier, which is a good sixty feet in the air. When a guard opened his door, he ran out and dove head first over the tier. I was just coming into the cell house when that happened. He lit on the concrete, not more than twenty feet from me, busting just about every bone in his body. The poor guy lived about six hours before he died. I felt so bad about that because the poor bastard didn't even know the guys were just kidding him. I hope to God the guys who kidded him felt bad too.

It seems like there was always a knifing; somebody was getting shivved, or their throat cut. I remember one very clearly. This young colored guy and a white boy worked in the main lobby as janitors. This colored guy was always after the young kid, giving him a bad time, and trying to make a girl out of him. The kid kept resisting his advances until one night, he had just all he could take. He jumped on the negro with a knife and ran him through that lobby cutting and slashing. The guards were getting out of the way. That kid literally cut that negro to pieces, which he had coming.

That is something I have never held within the penitentiary. There are so many who are naturally "gay", and they love the attention, so to force one's self on some poor kid who's weaker I've never believed in. I have always felt it was wrong but when a man is in the pen, he does his own time, and can't stick up for anybody. If he does, the "pack" is on him.

A lot of good people are in prison; people I'm proud to call friends. But there are some who if I had my way, I'd put them all in a room and turn the gas on. So many are so cold hearted that life means nothing to them, your life or their life; they'd just as soon kill you as look at you. They are no good to themselves, society, or anyone else and they don't deserve to live because they don't contribute anything to this world.

The best prison job I ever had was working on a tug boat which went from the island to the mainland. It pushed a barge that carried semi loads of finished material from the different industries on McNeil.

It was quite an experience for a man to be in a penitentiary and be a deck hand on a tug boat at the same time. During the summer it was a pretty good deal. I could lie out in the sun; there wasn't much work to do except tie up at the docks and drive the trucks on and off.

When winter came, Puget Sound got a little rough; the waves were pretty high. It was icy and cold on the tug boat but all in all, I really enjoyed it.

A one-legged sea gull would sit up on the front of the tug boat and keep all the other sea gulls away. That was his favorite roost and I guess he figured that was his tug boat. We had a baby seal too. It was sick and we nursed it back to health. That seal would follow the boat all the time, and even come up and lie on the deck until he got dry, then he would go back into the water. It was quite a pet; those big, soulful eyes would look at us and he was so cute. We couldn't help but love him.

It's a funny thing about a convict; with all the hell he's gone through, all the intimidation, and brutality, most of them are softhearted. I've seen guys sitting in a show, when they'd have a movie about a little kid or something, and they would start crying. I think that deep down inside convicts have more sympathy for the downtrodden than anyone I know.

I left McNeil for the last time in early '73, and went home to Red Lodge where I opened my own upholstery shop. Even then, I didn't know that alcohol was my main problem. I thought if I turned my life around and didn't break the law, that I could make out all right, especially since I had a trade and could make a good living out there.

CHAPTER 14

Free Time

I'd get out of these damn places and go back to raising hell, drinking, and stealing; anything to make a fast buck. I was on the move all the time from one place to another, never knowing where I would be next or if I'd be in jail. The law was looking for me most of the time. It's really not a good way to live. Every time someone went by my door and stopped, I'd wonder if it was the law. If a cop across the street looked in my direction, I'd wonder if he'd recognize me. I couldn't make any friends or have any close ties because I never knew when I'd have to pick up and leave.

My release from Leavenworth, the spring of '62, was no different than all the rest. I went to downtown Leavenworth, which has a population of 3500, to catch the bus into Kansas City. The thirty minutes I had before the bus left were spent in a beer joint across the street. Three beers hit me like a ton of bricks. When it was time for my bus to leave, I realized that I'd left my savings bonds at the joint. All the money I'd earned while working for the prison industries was in those savings bonds. I had to call a cab and go back after them.

By then, I'd missed my bus so the cab driver called for clearance to take me on into Kansas City. The fare was twenty dollars for the thirty-five-mile drive. He proceeded to tell me his troubles on the way into Kansas City; his wife had been with somebody else the night before and he was feeling pretty bad. I said, "Friend, now you have really got problems. The best thing that you can do is every time you see a cocktail or beer sign, stop this cab and we'll go in and have a few." By the time we got to Kansas City, I had a drunk cab driver on my hands.

I'd met some guys called "The Straw Hat Gang" while I was in Leavenworth. They were in for robbing Savings and Loans, and so forth. If I would pick them up, after I got out, they would give me five thousand dollars. I could sure use the money so I agreed to half down and the other half after I helped them escape. A girl friend of one of the gangs would furnish the car and pay me the twenty-five hundred down. After I got into Kansas City, I spent quite a bit of time running around looking for their address. That cost me about forty dollars in cab fare. I was pretty hot over the whole thing. They had fed me a snow job when I'd promised faithfully to help them. I'd stuck my neck out because I thought they were on the up and up.

I went out partying that night; after all I was locked up for quite a while and a man wants to get out and live a little bit. I met this woman in a nightclub, whose husband was doing time in Jefferson City, Missouri. She was having a hard time of it so I told her if she'd spend the evening with me, dining, dancing, and partying, I'd make it right with her. If she wished to stay the night with me, I would see that she was paid well and help her out as much as I could.

We went around to several nightclubs that night and I noticed she'd be talking to different guys. They'd look at me and I just had a feeling that before the night was over, they would try to rob me. I didn't have much money on me, about one-hundred and fifty dollars. The rest of my bonds weren't cashed yet. I kept on my toes but things went well throughout the evening.

After all the joints were closed, we ended up in the hotel of her choice. I picked up a fifth of whiskey, set it on the dresser, and stripped right down to my shorts. I was ready to make a little love but she kept stalling. The next thing I knew, she grabbed my billfold and took off out the door with it. I guess she'd assumed that since I was in my shorts, I'd stop and put my pants on before I took after her but she figured wrong. I chased her clear through the lobby of that hotel catching her at the front door. The clerk came running over and wanted to know what was wrong.

I told him, "No trouble at all. She just took my goddamn money and I'm going to get it back."

He said, "Well, I'll call the police."

I said, "To hell with the police. They don't have my money. She has."

I grabbed her and tore her dress off. She finally reached down inside her bra and handed my money back. Then she started to leave and I still felt sorry for her so I handed her twenty dollars. She walked out the door and I got to thinking about what a damn fool I was. I kicked her right square in the butt and damn near broke my foot. Then I went back up to my room and went to bed.

The next day I woke up sick and had to go to Chicago. I looked at that bottle and said, "To hell with you." I never even touched a drop. I left it sitting on the dresser and caught the bus to Chicago. But like any alcoholic, after I hit Chicago, I was partying again.

I threw in with another guy and we started robbing places but unfortunately, we picked the wrong places to rob. We were lying in our hotel room one morning, with a thirty-eight pistol and a sack of money by our bed, when two guys walked into the room. At first, I thought they were detectives. I made a grab for the gun but they got it first. I found out they were part of the mob. It seemed we had robbed one of their places, which they didn't appreciate, so they took us down to their hangout and had a talk with us. We were given two choices, either leave Chicago or be shipped out in a box. Naturally, we left in a hurry. They had been very polite about it and weren't interested in calling the police because they took care of their own.

We went to Detroit for a while doing the same thing; stickups. I was very proficient and convincing with a gun, and usually got what I wanted. A lot of the time, I got what I didn't want! I never shot anybody; I never had to or wanted to. The most dreadful thing about being a stick-up man was the fear that someday I might have to pull the trigger on some innocent person. When I was robbing somebody, there was no right. I would be wrong no matter what happened. Even if I defended myself and shot someone, I'd still be wrong.

I worked my way West from Detroit, drinking all the way. I can't remember many of the things I've done while drinking. More than likely I never would see the outside of a prison if I'd been picked up on them. It seemed like every time I woke up sick, I'd vow never to take another drink but I always did.

When I got as far as Montana, I stopped to visit my mother for a few days. I wasn't getting along too well with her so I left for Idaho. Well, that was my downfall. The authorities picked me up in Caldwell, Idaho for violation of parole. I'd been drinking and robbed this store in Twin Falls, Idaho. I was sent to McNeil for my first stay.

As soon as I was released, I went back to RedLodge for a while. I didn't have a trade and work was hard to find so I left for Billings. That got me a year and a half sentence to DeerLodge. I'd already been there in '49 and '56. Writing bad checks or forging someone else's seemed to be my weakness when I was drinking. That time I got it for forgery.

Denver was my next stop after I got out of DeerLodge. I met some Mexican girl who traveled around the country with me. I was hustling and stealing all the time. She finally left me somewhere down in California.

I ran California from one end to the other, with a pistol, robbing places. I'll never forget the time I robbed this theatre. A young girl was taking tickets. I threw down on her with police positive 38 and told her to give me the money. She was scared and kept handing me rolls of pennies. I was trying to tell her I didn't want the pennies; Finally, I got disgusted and left on the run. I damn near got caught in San Francisco over a few pennies.

It is surprising what a man can do with a pistol; it is also surprising how much time he can get. My freedom came to an end in Idaho.

The law picked me up for burglary in Boise. That time I was released into the custody of a United States Marshal for five years. Had I kept myself clean, another prison term would have been avoided. But I didn't and was picked up for violation of the Dyer Act, which is a term the FBI tacked onto interstate transportation of a stolen vehicle. That got me my second round in McNeil, and I wasn't paroled until I served three of five years.

Some of the really good, or I guess I should say big things that I've done, I've gotten away with. As long as I left the booze alone while I was capering, I never had any trouble. When I was half drunk, it seemed like

I always got caught. When a man rebels, drinks, and don't change his ways, he just goes from one trouble to another. My time as a free man has always been short-lived. I think my longest time without any violation of the law was a bit over three years. By luck, I was able to land a good job and even though I continued drinking, I held onto it for quite a while.

CHAPTER 15

Pappy's First Good Job

My training in McNeil finally paid off. I'd become a top-notch upholsterer. My little shop in the basement of RedLodge's Old Chief Hotel was doing quite well, but I got a chance at a job that offered travel, a fantastic wage and benefit package and I was always ready for some adventure. A friend of mine had received some papers from Lear Siegler, Inc., which is affiliated with Lear Jet. They wanted him to go to work and he didn't want to go so I filled those papers out and sent them in. Lear Siegler handled repair, maintenance, and supply contracts for the Air Force. They were redoing some of the Air Force radar planes and needed someone who could do upholstery work on the seats in those planes.

The next thing I knew, I received a long-distance call from them. They wanted me to report to Otis Air Force Base in Massachusetts and start work. I dropped everything and left for Massachusetts. This was the first good job I'd ever had and nobody cared whether I was an ex-convict or not. It was rather hard to believe that I was going to get a break in my life but I did.

I was there for about two months when they needed me at the Little Rock, Arkansas Air Base. The company would pay all my travel expenses and I would receive so much a day for living expenses plus my hourly wage. Four of us, all close friends, went to the job in Little Rock.

They were replacing wing panels in bombers that had stress cracks in them. We were working fourteen to sixteen hours a day, seven days a week, so we didn't have much time left for ourselves, but it seemed like I always had time to drink.

The American Legion Club had a band every night so we spent our off time there. We'd drink and dance, then get home just in time to go to work. All we kept in the icebox at home was booze. Four of us shared a four-bedroom apartment. After work, we'd have a few drinks then maybe go out and have some supper, but we always ended up at the American Legion Club.

I met quite a few ladies at the club who liked to dance. Most of them were divorced or widowed, and like me, they were lonely; in fact, like any ex- con because we are all lonely. I took the women out and danced with them. I liked one in particular very much, but made the mistake of marrying her. Noreen and I were married in '68 right after my forty-fourth birthday. By the time a man is that age he should know better than to marry an exact opposite and that's what we were; we had nothing in common.

Noreen was very religious and she had a lot of problems that were caused by rheumatoid arthritis. Eventually our love cooled but not the love I had for my stepdaughters.

Noreen had two daughters, Dee Dee and Omie, and a son who was a marine stationed in Vietnam. I tried to make a life for Dee Dee and Omie; I probably didn't do all that I could have but I really tried because I loved them.

Noreen and I lived in Little Rock and I stayed on at the base. We'd gone to Hot Springs on a short honeymoon. Several months after we were married, my contract at the base was up, so I decided to take my wife and stepdaughters back to Montana to meet my mother. We didn't even stay a week because nothing went right from the time we got there. I made the mistake of taking Noreen to a birthday party while we were in Red Lodge. She became extremely jealous of an old girlfriend and caused such a scene that we had to leave. Then too, my mother didn't even try to get along with Noreen and the girls. Noreen wanted to do the cooking so my mother wouldn't have so much to do, but Mother criticized everything she did. Noreen said she was too possessive of me and jealous of her and the kids. Mother said she couldn't understand Noreen's Arkansas accent. I finally went uptown and got drunk and while I was out of the house, my mother proceeded to tell Noreen about my past. I knew nothing about their conversation and couldn't figure out why Noreen acted so cold and distant on our trip back to Little Rock.

When we got back to Little Rock, I contacted Lear Siegler again but it would have been two or three months before they had anything. I finally found a job with an outfit that upholstered church pews. While I was working for them my mother came for a visit. She had planned to stay at least two weeks but her and Noreen started having quarrels, again. I overheard my mother telling Noreen about my past so I went and got drunk. A couple of hours later, I came back and caused a big scene. Mother's visit only lasted a week but she accomplished what she came for because things were never the same between my wife and I after that.

Right after my mother left, Little Rock Airmotive began hiring. They paid a higher wage that the outfit I was with so I went to work for them. I'd been with the other outfit approximately a month when I decided to make the switch. Little Rock Airmotive was in the business of customizing executive jets. I designed seats and did all of their interior upholstery. I stayed with them until Lear Siegler called me five months later.

Lear Siegler wanted me to come up to Midwest City, which is located right out of Oklahoma City, for an interview. They asked if I was interested in going to work in Vietnam. Besides the money they paid, I'd had about all I could take of Noreen. I didn't know if I could go or not because I was an ex-con but I put in for it and was accepted.

While working for the company I had to have security clearance but in order to go to Vietnam, I had to have secret service clearance. There was no one more surprised than I when the FBI cleared me. It seemed like the only thing they were interested in was whether or not I was or ever had been a communist. I had to fill out papers and there must have been a hundred different organizations that were communist affiliated. I had to check each one and tell whether I'd belonged to it or not. Needless to say, I'd never been a communist and at the end of the paper I put down, "I have never been a communist; in fact, it's all I can do to be an American. I bet they got a laugh out of that.

I prepared to go to Vietnam and told my wife and daughters, "Don't worry, I'll make good money and everything will be all right." I had to fly to San Francisco and wait there about two weeks before flying from Travis Air Force Base to Vietnam.

The guys I worked with were all ex-GIs or had retired from the military. We were all heavy drinkers and partied the entire two weeks we were in San Francisco. The night we left for Vietnam, everyone on the plane was drunk and we all had booze with us.

The flight to Vietnam took about seventeen hours. We landed at Tan Son Nhut Air Base. When we arrived, the base was under mortar attack so we couldn't land and had to circle for a while. When we did come in, we had to come fast and low; then the plane had to get out of there right away.

Forty-eight civilians were on the plane with us. Out of those forty-eight, ten decided they were going back to the States right then. I guess they hadn't realized quite what they were getting into. I'd experienced many hardships in my life so it was nothing to get shot at, live in a tent, or rough it like any GI.

I was very fortunate because Lear Siegler used my Honorable Discharge and ignored the Dishonorable, I'd gotten when I was in Hawaii. They classified me as a GS9 which is a civilian rank equivalent to a Major in the service. This rating gave me all the privileges of an officer including the Officers Club.

Vietnam

My first station in Vietnam was a place called Phouc Le which was an Air Chopper Base for Cobra Gun Ships. The Viet Cong hated them because they were armed with Mini-guns, fashioned after the old Gatling Gun of the Cavalry. On one pass over a football field the Cobra could put a bullet in every square foot of it. The Viet Cong would hit the air base with rockets, mortar and ground attacks, anything to get to those helicopter gun ships and destroy them. We could see the guns in action at night and they would look like a river of fire was coming out of them. They were a terrible weapon.

I really enjoyed Vietnam because it was kind of like being back in the service and I guess that deep down inside I'd always wanted to go back into the service. I'm just an old GI at heart so no matter how bad things got, I could take them in stride.

Booze was very cheap and we could buy the best at the PX for two dollars a quart. Most of the time I was half bombed and like everyone else stayed that way so the tension wouldn't bother me. I still couldn't convince myself that I was an alcoholic and it would seem that after all the years filled with crazy things, I'd done that I would have realized my biggest problem was alcohol. It had gotten me into more trouble than anything else. Every time I'd gone to jail, I was drunk; not that I didn't commit many of my crimes when I was sober.

When I had come out of Angola, I'd made up my mind to defy authority in every way possible. Robbing and living by my wits; not bragging or anything but I was a damn good thief when I left the booze alone, but when I'd get drunk, I'd run out of money and write bad checks. I wasn't even smart enough to use someone else's name on them. Hell, I'd sign my own. I guess I was trying to punish myself, trying to put myself back in prison and I've often wondered if that was the case or not but I do believe it very well could have been. Actually, Vietnam probably kept me out of prison for a while.

My first time over in Vietnam (July of 1968) I tried to see my wife's son who was in the Marines but he was on the forward bases and I never did get to meet him.

When my plane landed in Vietnam that first time, I stayed in an old hotel, or I guess that's what it was, in Saigon. I had a room with a fan in it and a kind of company toilet. The first night, I was sitting out on the patio and dozed off. Some little Vietnamese stole my glasses and without them I'm nearly blind. For two months I couldn't even do my work so I just drew my pay and did nothing until I finally got some glasses from the States.

There were so many kids running the streets who had no home, no people, and nothing to eat. Their families were killed in the war or displaced and those kids had to steal to survive so if you wore a wrist watch, you wouldn't have it for long. One of those kids would come by, snatch it off your wrist, and be gone with it. I lost mine twice but the first time managed to ransom it back. The second time, it was gone for good, and I felt bad about it because it had belonged to my stepfather. It was one of the few things I had to remember him by but no matter how hard I tried; I couldn't get it back.

When we left Saigon for Phouc Le, about twenty-two miles out, we went by truck. They drove like a bat out of hell because of sniper fire. We never could tell when someone would take a shot at us from one of the villages we went through.

Phouc Le was quite a base with plenty of booze and our ration was eight quarts a month. I had an "in" with the sergeant who ran the NCO Club so I could get all the booze I wanted and kept myself pretty well supplied. The company didn't care if we drank as long as we did our job.

The officers had a swimming pool, they'd built and paid for themselves, and it was pretty nice. The first Fourth of July we were there, we civilians decided to throw a party for the officers and the men we worked with so we took over their swimming pool. We had plenty of booze, plenty to eat and a lot of Vietnamese girls. Well, the party ended in a drunken brawl with everyone throwing everyone else in the pool. I'm a little guy and it seemed like every time I'd try to throw someone in, I'd end up in it myself. I was thrown in at least ten times.

When I was ready to leave the party, my friend gave me a ride home on his Honda motorcycle. We were both drunk. I got on the back and he said, "Are you ready?" I said, "Yeah," and boy did he take off. I went off the back end; after I got back on again, off we went down the road. We were going around a corner and there came a damn jeep which ran us off the road. We went through some barbed wire and finally stopped. We were standing out there drunker than hell, holding onto that motorcycle. Everyone was hollering at us, including the MP's, telling us to stand right where we were which was right in the middle of a mine field. We didn't give a damn and couldn't hear anyway, or at least didn't care whether we did or not. We actually pushed that motorcycle out of the mine field and never set a mine off! They couldn't believe it.

We got back on again and took off for our hooch which was in the backend of some aircraft hangars. Rather than go all the way around the hangars, he decided to cut right through. There were big doors in the front but a small door in the back, about as wide as a house door, maybe not even that wide. We went through the front, going like hell, right past a bunch of GIs who were working on aircraft. They scattered in every direction and how we ever got through the back door I'll never know because I didn't think that motorcycle would fit.

Eight of us lived in a hooch which was a tent with a board floor, board sidewalls, and sandbagged all the way around. In case of a mortar or rocket attack the schrapnel wouldn't pass through the sandbags. In case of a direct hit, they didn't do much good.

We had two portable Japanese ice boxes filled with nothing but booze and one can of fruit cocktail. The fruit cocktail was for our Mynah bird. He was almost human and cantankerous so whenever we'd lay down to read or something, he'd continually pester us. He would pull our ears, pick at the paper and just plain torment us because he was always wanting attention.

Whenever anyone would open up the icebox, he would be right there after that can of fruit cocktail. He didn't want us to give him a piece but wanted to help himself. He'd get on the end of the can, bury his head in there and pick out what he wanted. If I had a mixed drink on the table, he would have his head in that so he spent most of his time intoxicated. He would pick up any cigarette that was lying around and walk around with it in his beak like he was smoking it.

One guy in our tent didn't like this bird so every time the bird had to take a crap, he'd fly over this man's bed and do it, then he'd fly up to the top of the tent where nobody could get to him. That guy used to get so damned mad he couldn't see straight but there was nothing he could do because he knew how much we thought of that Mynah bird. He didn't dare touch him.

We had a Mama-san to take care of our hooch. She would wash our clothes, shine our shoes, and make our beds for six dollars a month. We were getting twenty-eight dollars a day for living expenses plus our wages. We ate in the mess hall and our meals cost us twenty-five cents so our expenses were not very much.

Right outside of Phouc Le, by the main gate there was a building with a sign that said, "Laundry" which was the local whorehouse. That's where we all went. It was off limits to GIs but the MPs couldn't touch us civilians. We carried Mack B identification and non-combatant cards. Now the non-combatant card was quite a thing. It had our picture, name and occupation on it. If the North Vietnamese overran the base, we were supposed to show them that card and let them know we were not soldiers. Now you can imagine me holding a card up to a North Vietnamese coming at me with a rifle or bayonet, trying to explain to him that I'm not a soldier! Like hell I would. We all carried side arms and if they'd overrun the base we'd have been right there fighting with the GIs. We were all ex-GIs anyway.

We would go to this whorehouse to get the Mama-san and her girls. The girls were clean because they had to keep them clean. The venereal rate was very high in Vietnam and they checked the girls all the time. The civilians that worked at the base and the Vietnamese men were checked medically to make sure they had no venereal disease because if they had it, it would spread all through the army. In Saigon and other places, the girls weren't so lucky. Most of them were dosed up; therefore, we were darn particular about who we fooled with.

I had a favorite girl at the laundry. Since the girls slept on a woven grass mat, I'd always end up with skinned knees and elbows from making love. It was pretty hard to get used to.

We would sit around Mama-san's drinking Bombity Bomb beer and try to out lie each other. Mama-san took in orphan kids; she had a heart which was almost as big as all of the outdoors. One boy had a crooked leg; he'd had rickets at one time and it had crippled him. He took a shine to me and I to him so whenever I'd go into the local village to buy things, he'd go with me. Well, he was my manager. Whenever they had a price for anything he'd argue like hell and jew them down until the price was right. He'd never let anybody take advantage of me. He was my favorite and I paid for all of his food and clothing while I was over in Vietnam.

Mama-san also had a little big-eyed girl who was very serious, quiet, and never spoke. Mama-san told me that her people were killed right before her eyes. Every time I went to the laundry, I'd take her some candy or gum. She would always accept it and look at me but never talk. She would sit up on my lap snuggling as close as she could.

I will never forget the day I came to see Mama-san and the girls; that little girl came running up to me, threw her arms around me and started jabbering. Mama-san told me that she was calling me Papa in Vietnamese and telling me how much she loved me. I had brought her back out of the deep depression she was experiencing in her own world. She was back in reality but I've often wondered if she wasn't better off in her own world than in the reality of Vietnam. At least then, I felt better about her speaking.

The Viet Cong attacked the base one night by coming in through the dump. A friend and I were drinking so we moved as close as we could to watch the Cobra guns firing back. We had a bottle sitting up on a rock and we were on the ground. Every once in a while, we would see a red streak go by. My friend said, "What's that?". I said, "Hell, I suppose it's tracers." And he said, "Jesus Christ, get that bottle down 'for they hit it!" We worried more about that bottle than we did about ourselves. Finally, the MPs came over and ran us off. They called us crazy civilians, which we were.

I started living with a girl in Saigon on the weekends. I'd fly in for the weekend and go back to the base on Monday morning. Her name was Kim and she was a doll. She looked just like one of those little China dolls we used to put on the bed. I met her on one of my weekends in Saigon. We stayed at a hotel that had a swimming pool and bar on the roof and naturally we spent most of our time there.

Saigon Tea girls worked there and made money off the drinks they sold. We would buy them Saigon Tea, a little cup about the size of a shot glass, which wasn't anything but cold tea and everyone knew it. It cost us one-hundred piastre which is about the equivalent to twenty cents, American money. They got so many piastre for every drink they sold.

Of course, they had whiskey and American beer and an American whiskey. They had a Vietnamese Beer called Thirty-Three and that's what we called Bombity Bomb beer. It was rumored that they aged it with formaldehyde and believe me, it would make us drunk and also give us some of the worst hangovers we'd ever had. Well, I met Kim at this hotel where she worked as a Tea Girl.

The Tea Girls would stay with a man for about twenty dollars a night, American money. Ten of that would go to Mama-san who was the head woman over the girls. I guess five went to the hotel and five to the girl. Mama-san always kept the girls in debt so they never came out ahead. Eventually, Kim and I got an apartment in the Chlon district of Saigon which was the Chinese district. It was a tough place but I was never bothered. I was respected by the Vietnamese and Chinese because I understood their ways and tried to learn their customs.

Our apartment cost us sixty dollars a month and it was a small room with a community bath and no shower. What I would do was squat and Kim would pour water over me. That was quite an experience; to have a woman pouring a bucket of water over me, especially since she was giving me a bath.

The Vietnamese are a very clean people so every time we made love, we'd have to take a bath. For a while I took quite a few baths. I got so that I knew if I wanted to make love, I was going to have to take a bath so I slowed down a bit. But I spent every weekend with Kim, then I'd fly back to Phouc Le.

I have wished many times over that I'd brought her back with me. If I'd realized that my wife and I were eventually going to be divorced I would have. Kim would wait on me hand and foot and take care of my every need. When I'd wake up in the morning, she'd have my coffee for me and she loved me all the time; in fact, she really spoiled me.

I know I wasn't true to my wife but I felt there wasn't anything between us anymore. I loved my little stepdaughters, though, and that is the reason I hadn't divorced her. I felt they needed a father and I really needed them; someone I could have close to me, care about, and who cared about me. I sent them Chinese gowns and robes, with the slit on the side, made of silk. They would get all dressed up and were really cute.

Saigon had a curfew which started at six in the evening and lifted at six in the morning. Some of the guys used to ride their motorbikes into Saigon. They weren't to go into Saigon during the curfew hours at all and were told that they were taking their life in hand between those hours, but they'd go anyway. One day they ran right into the middle of a fire fight between the North Vietnamese and some GIs. Several of them were shot but not killed; even that failed to stop them. Those that were still able continued their trips to Saigon via motorcycle at all hours.

Our first real casualty on base happened in an odd way. The guy was sitting on the privy at about four in the morning. He probably had a touch of the trots. Some rockets came in sending a piece of shrapnel through the back of the privy. He must have been wiping his behind because he lost a piece of his fanny and two fingers.

Some civilians, working at the forward base, were captured by the North Vietnamese. We never heard anymore from them although a few of them returned after the war as POWS.

I had quite a few close calls while I was in Vietnam. I was shot at a few times in Saigon and I'd just left one place when it was bombed. That was really close but I also had some good times as I began to understand the people. They had nothing and I used to feel sorry for their way of life because they didn't have a thing and never expected anything. Their families were close; they loved their children and took care of their old people, some things most Americans don't do. I tried to learn their culture and became very close friends with a Vietnamese family.

The man had three sons and he offered me one of them to bring back to the states. He knew his son would get an education and there would be a future for him. Unfortunately, I couldn't accept because of the expense and all of the red tape that I would have to go through to get anything done. I have often wished that I could have done that one favor for him and his oldest son. He was a good man and loved his family enough to be willing to sacrifice one son, to do that much for one of his boys.

We went to the NCO Club often and that used to make the officers mad. We were considered officers and they wanted our patronage at their club. Well, they were a bunch of stuffed shirts. We couldn't enjoy ourselves when we went down there so we'd go to drink their booze, eat their food, then go back to the NCO Club and really get drunk.

When we would get to the NCO Club, we'd put money up on the bar and drink until it was gone; naturally we were pretty popular. I really had a ball; there isn't anything like going with a bunch of enlisted men when I'd been one myself. Some of the GIs were jealous of us civilians because of the money we made but they did realize that we too had our butts on the line, the same as they did. We had just as good a chance of getting killed too.

I had some good times at Phouc Le. A colonel was in charge of the base who believed that all of his senior NCOs and all of his officers could keep women on base, but he wouldn't let the lower ranking men do it. We were sitting around the hooch drinking one night with this old supply sergeant, a relic from World War II, who could get anything we wanted. We mentioned we should get some girls in and throw a party. We went and got a ton and a half truck, then loaded up a bunch of Vietnamese whores and sneaked them back in. We threw a party and believe me; it was a party! Most everyone was running around naked, raising hell and getting drunk. We turned a bunch of girls over to the GIs. Well, about three o'clock in the morning, they woke the Colonel up. Three of the GIs and three girls were in the Officer's shower taking a bath and that's what woke him up.

We had outside showers rigged up but with the water over there, we never could get clean. It had a kind of rust in it, so what we'd do during the rainy season was go out into the company street and take a shower in the rain.

I was doing that one night and when I was through started back into the hooch when one of the guys took a picture of me. I had nothing on and was holding a bar of soap in my hand. They had a bunch of prints made up and tacked them up all over the outfit. I was called the Streaker. I did look funny as hell naked with nothing but a bar of soap in my hand, but anything for a laugh over there. We'd do all kinds of things that guys would not normally do just for the laugh we got.

During my last tour of Vietnam which began during the winter of '68, I went to Qui Nhon where I was stationed at An Khe. (I stayed for thirteen months without going back to the States.) Qui Nhon is at the very southern end of Vietnam. We had a contract to set up supply and maintenance for the 241st Tank Command. Believe me it was a mess; they had a base there but it was so disorganized that we had to inventory everything.

Every two weeks I would take a convoy of trucks nonstop, with all GIs except me, and make deliveries to Phu Cat, Phu Son, Chu Lai, and Phu Bai. From Chu Lai to Phu Bai we usually drew small sniper fire and occasionally artilary fire. We were loaded with aircraft parts going up and empty coming back. Tanks and armor went ahead to clear our way of obstacles but it was still a pretty hairy trip.

We'd stop for nothing or no one in our way. If a truck became disabled, the driver and guards were picked up and the rest was left for the rear guards to retrieve. Many times, the bridges would be blown up and temporary ones were put up to get us through.

Qui Nhon was off limits to GIs but we civilians would go in there. It was pretty much of a hot spot too. I went into the Neptune Bar and a few other places there but I had to watch out because the Viet Cong would go into a bar and leave a satchel charge. When the damn thing would go off it would blow the bar and everyone in it all to hell. One day I was sitting in a bar and heard an explosion; the Viet Cong had placed a satchel charge in a theater up the street which was full of women and kids. I went up and helped as much as I could carrying out the wounded and what was left of them. It made me so damn mad! The poor civilians had to suffer all the god-damned pain. Why blow-up civilians instead of the men that were fighting the war? The poor little kids never done anything.

When we went to Vietnam, we started hiring Vietnamese and paying them an equivalent of sixty dollars a month in American currency. This was a hell of a lot more than they'd ever been used to but like every place we go into, we try to turn it into the American way of life. That is the worst thing in the world to do to people who never had anything and never wanted anything because they never had anything to want. We ruin every country we ever go into with our good deeds, kindness, and good heartedness. Instead of trying to learn their way of life and do things the way they do them, we have to change everybody in this world to our way and we just can't do it.

The Vietnamese took care of their elderly until they learned that they could use them too, for survival in the war. They would take the old folks that were of no use anymore, couldn't work or anything and stand up with them alongside the road. When a truck would come, they would push them out in front of it. If a GI ran over one of them the family could collect a bounty which was eighty dollars in American money. It was cruel but it was survival. A typical Vietnamese family lived on the equivalent of sixty dollars, American money, a year.

There was a "Cat House" just across from the base at Qui Nhon. Some of us would go over there and spend the night but it was off limits to the GIs. The MPs saw to that. The GIs would get so damn mad that they'd stand across the road and throw rocks on the roof all night trying to keep us awake. They didn't bother us because the Vietnamese burned some kind of incense and we didn't sleep too well anyway. It would stick to our clothes and skin; we could smell it for weeks afterwards.

It may sound like I was over in Vietnam for a long time but I wasn't; I spent a total of nineteen months there. I came back to the States after my first six months was up (winter of '68) but things weren't going right so I decided to go back over to Vietnam again. For every six-month contract we'd get a bonus to sign up for another six months and then after eighteen months, we'd get all our income tax back which amounted to quite a bit.

While I was in Vietnam, my wife would get one hundred fifty dollars a week and I was clearing around two thousand a month. I sent money home for her to put in the bank because I wanted to open my own business when I returned. I figured that I had about eighteen thousand saved but on my last return home I had six hundred, in the bank and divorce papers. My wife had spent it all on her Arkansas relatives, so the nineteen months I spent in Vietnam were a waste of time.

I have many good memories of Vietnam. I really loved those people; they were straightforward in their ways and sure they stole and did many things to survive, but it was understandable.

CHAPTER 17

Back In the States Again

I returned to the States in January of 1970. By that March, I was on my way back to the pen. The plane I came back on flew from Tan Son Nhut to Kobe, Japan. We were all detained for seven hours while the plane was searched. I never did find out why except that it was either for a bomb or drugs. After the Air Force plane landed at Travis Air Base, in California, I called Noreen. She seemed excited but I found out later that she was scared. From Travis, I caught a commercial flight to Little Rock. No one was waiting at the airport so I took a taxi home.

I was in for quite a surprise when I got there; my wife had spent almost eighteen thousand dollars on her Arkansas relatives. All I got out of my time in Vietnam was six-hundred dollars and a divorce. I sure couldn't open my own upholstery shop on either. I didn't mind the divorce we weren't getting along anyway, but I'd have given her what was fair out of my savings, so she didn't have to rip me off. I had trusted Noreen because she was very religious. The thought that she'd steal from me never entered my head.

Noreen did let me have her new car but it wasn't paid for. I took my clothes and left. Why I went to Albuquerque, New Mexico, I will never know. I'd spent about four days with a group of college students drinking, smoking pot, and making love when the FBI picked me up. The United States Marshall wanted me back in Little Rock for forging a government check. The law took me back to Little Rock; my new car stayed in Albuquerque.

The check happened to be a friend's income tax return. This friend was one of the three guys who'd shared my apartment when I first moved to Little Rock. One night when we'd all been out partying, he'd asked me to sign his name to it because he was too drunk; then he didn't remember asking me or even spending it. When my hearing came up, this so-called friend testified that he'd never seen the check and my lawyer couldn't locate the other two guys who'd been with us. That got me my second and last sentence to Leavenworth.

While I was waiting to be transported to Leavenworth, Noreen came, not to see me, but to have me sign my five-hundred-dollar income tax refund check. She said she needed it for the girls; knowing that I'd sign it for them but not for her.

After I'd been in Leavenworth two years, I bugged out and stabbed a guy so they transferred me to McNeil Island. They had closed Alcatraz by then, but they warned me that if I didn't straighten up my act that my next stop would be Marion, Illinois. Marion was built to house the most dangerous convicts after Alcatraz was closed.

McNeil wasn't a bad place to be. They let me have plenty of freedom as long as I behaved myself, which I did. I went back to doing upholstery for a while, then worked as a trustee on the prison farm, and on the tug boat. When I was released in '73, it was on what they call mandatory release. That's about the same as parole.

Pierce Packing, a Billings firm, was hiring when I went back to Montana. Instead of going to RedLodge, I decided to try something different for a while. Me and a bunch of Polacks hung beef in railroad boxcars. I'd unhook a beef side, throw it over my shoulder, and carry it into the boxcar where I had to hang it on another hook. Some of those sides of beef weighed over three-hundred pounds. I spent more time crawling out from underneath them than I did carrying them, but I finally got onto the knack of how to distribute their weight. I was there several weeks when Pierce Packing transferred me to the position of inventory clerk. I would keep track of production for each day.

I soon tired of working at the packing plant and moved back to RedLodge. Mother was renting a small house in which I opened an upholstery shop. There wasn't much room for me to work but I made out okay. Lear Siegler surprised me with a call about a month after I'd moved back home. They wanted me to work for them in Tampa, Florida. It didn't take me long to close shop and head for Florida. I went to work at McDill Air Force base modifying fuel tanks for planes. They had to be pressure checked and so forth to ensure safety.

After I was there approximately six months, I met Rose Rhodes and started shaking up with her. She had money and was an alcoholic so we made a good pair. When I was transferred to San Bernardino, California, on another Air Force contract, she went with me. I lost my job in San Bernardino because of booze so we decided to stop in RedLodge to see my mother on our way back to Florida.

We were home three days when she got drunk and we had a big fight, over some woman I'd talked to in the bar. As soon as we got in the door at Mother's Rose grabbed a butcher knife and tried to stab me in the stomach. I knocked her over the coffee table and broke a ceramic bird that had belonged to my grandmother. Mother was all upset and started yelling so I packed Rose up and left for Florida.

On the way back, I got as far as Murfeesboro, Tennessee when I gave in and called Alcoholics Anonymous. By then, I didn't know where I was and couldn't even find my car. They took me to a halfway house where I stayed for a couple of weeks. Mother was notified; she sent plane fare so I could get home.

I managed to get a job upholstering booths for a bar owner when I got back to RedLodge. We made a deal on how much the job was going to cost but he tried to finagle out of it. Mother was after me all the time because I wasn't charging enough for my work; she said I was just giving it away. I had the keys to this guy's bar so one day, when I went to work, I started drinking instead of doing upholstery. I got a pretty good snoot full, opened the till, took the money, and left in my station wagon.

Five miles west of Buffalo, Wyoming, my car went off the road and hit a boulder about the size of a house. I was doing about eighty-five when everything came to a sudden halt. The force of impact put the engine clear into the back seat. When I came too, I couldn't talk because my lower teeth were hanging out the bottom of my chin. One tooth was knocked out of my upper plate but my glasses were still on. An ambulance was called from Buffalo; before they could get to me, I got out and started walking towards it. The doctor who was on call sewed my chin up then I asked to be transferred on to the Vets hospital in Sheridan. I had four broken ribs and a punctured lung; the lung collapsed after I was in the Vets hospital. I stayed there about three weeks.

That was my second bad car accident. Twenty years or so before that, I bought a second-hand Pontiac in Red Lodge and was on my way to Washington when I had the other one. It had a faulty muffler so I stopped in Big Timber to get that fixed and bought a pint of whiskey. I had a cousin who lived in Butte and I had planned on seeing her when I went through town. I started over Butte Mountain, on the old highway which is full of switchbacks, and I was doing about a hundred. I made two of those switchbacks but that was all; my car broke and sailed through the guard rail two- hundred feet down the side of that mountain. I blacked out when it hit and woke up sometime in the night. One headlight was shining up into the sky and the radio was playing "Hang Down Your Head Tom Dooley". Somehow, I managed to crawl through the brush, up to the highway. A guy took me into the hospital. I called my cousin from there and she came and got me. It took me about ten days to recuperate but my car was junk.

While I was in the Vet's hospital, the Red Lodge sheriff sent one of his deputies up to question me. I told him exactly what happened, and that I knew I'd done wrong. But I told him I was angry, bitter, and drunk, or it wouldn't have happened. Had the man treated me fairly everything would have been all right. Mother borrowed money to reimburse the bar owner and the charges were dropped.

After I got out of the hospital, I bought an old Junker for a hundred dollars and headed for home. That broke down near Hardin so I sold it for a quarter and hitchhiked the rest of the way. Once again, I started doing upholstery work in RedLodge.

Mother had a chance to buy a small house from a good friend who was in a rest home in Columbus, Montana. We took a five-thousand-dollar savings certificate my stepfather had left us and bought the house. It needed a hell of a lot of work done on it so I started remodeling. I paneled it throughout and laid all the carpets. I even put a new roof on it.

A professional carpenter helped me put a new ceiling in my mother's bedroom. I converted the garage into a shop. I was really enjoying myself.

My mother backed me in my business so she wanted the checks made out to her. She would put them in the bank and pay our bills. If I needed a dollar, I'd have to ask for it and tell her what it was for. She didn't know anything about upholstery prices so after a while, I decided to make out two bills; one would be for the customer and I'd give her the fake one. If the material was ten dollars a yard and the customer needed five yards for a chair, his bill would be fifty dollars but the one I gave Mother was usually ten to fifteen dollars less. The only way that scheme worked was with cash paying customers so I tried to get them to pay cash most of the time. I'd tell my mother they didn't have a checking account. That way I had a little spending money and I didn't have to tell her anything about how I spent it or who I spent it on.

Still, my mother was a lot of fun to be with. I would often take her out to supper and dancing. What embarrassed me more than anything else was her paying for our drinks or else slipping the money under the table to me so I could pay for them. That made me feel like a little kid. Many times, I tried to sit down and relate to her about different things but I never got anywhere. When my stepfather was alive, he and I could always communicate.

Mother would say things that made me mad but she was getting old and I owed her a lot, so I tried to ignore her remarks; usually, I'd just turn to the bottle. But one morning, I couldn't take her constant criticism anymore. She'd just gotten out of the hospital after another nervous relapse and she was worse than ever. I threw a few clothes in my pickup and left. I only had about sixty dollars on me because I'd fully intended to go to the Veteran's Hospital in Sheridan, Wyoming and go through their alcoholic program.

I got almost to Sheridan when I picked up two hitchhikers who were going to Florida. Like a damn fool, I drove them all the way. We were close to Tampa when I suggested that we get a motel and rest. I'd driven most of the way from Wyoming and wanted to be more alert before driving into Tampa. During the night, they got up and left with my truck.

I reported it to the police and stayed on at the motel for several days while they tried to locate it. My money was practically all gone. The motel operator was raising hell over a couple of days lodging. He had me put in jail for attempting to defraud an innkeeper but when I explained the situation to the judge, the next morning, he let me out. A friend, in Red Lodge wired me enough money to pay the motel bill so I could get my clothes. Since I could no longer stay there, I took the bus on into Tampa and went to work as a day laborer. The Tampa police had my address in case my pickup was found. Seventeen days later, they notified me that they'd recovered it fifty miles from Tampa. Unfortunately for me, they'd found it three days after it was stolen but didn't notify me. It took my entire paycheck for that week just to pay the storage on my truck.

I finally earned enough money to drive back to Red Lodge. On the way back, I picked up two kids who were going to work on a ranch near Rawlins, Wyoming. We got as far as Glenwood Springs, Colorado before I was broke and low on gas. I told them we'd have to find a job washing dishes before we could go on. I went to different restaurants looking for work. Supposedly, they did the same thing and couldn't find anything. I suggested that we go back to Denver and look for work there. We got in the truck and were starting out of Glenwood Springs when four police cars pulled up alongside us; all the officers had their guns drawn. They scared the hell out of me. Come to find out, my pickup was still on the stolen list.

While I was trying to explain that the registration and title were in the glove box, one of them found a CB radio under the truck seat. I swore to God that I knew nothing about it. We were fingerprinted and booked into jail. Neither of the boys had a record but when mine came back, my goose was cooked. The kids owned up to stealing the radio out of somebody's car; they were going to sell it. We were in jail about thirty days when I told the kids there wasn't any use fighting it. I'd thought it was just a misdemeanor. The judge turned them loose and gave me nine months in the county jail. Mother was telling everyone that I was in the hospital in Denver; she was always covering up when I was in jail. I had the run of the place cooking for the other inmates. When my time was up, I headed for RedLodge and went back into the upholstery business again.

In '77, I met a real nice lady and planned on marrying her in the spring of 1978. Mother was jealous of Joanne; in fact, she was jealous of any of my women friends because I was the only thing she had left. She'd lost my stepfather, grandmother, and both of her brothers.

Mother would tell Joanne that I wasn't going to marry her. Joanne seldom came over to the house because of her remarks. Joanne was a Catholic girl and Mother didn't approve of that either. Joanne and I took a trip over to Cooke City. That upset my mother because she wanted me to take her instead of Joanne. Whenever we'd go to Billings on a shopping trip, Mother would go along; she always insisted on sitting next to me which ruined the trips for Joanne and me.

I wish today that those trips were all that was ruined. Joanne and I never got married. I was planning on spending the evening with her the night I killed my mother.

CHAPTER 18

Prelude to Murder

February 10, 1978, was my mother's seventy-fifth birthday. I took her out to supper and afterwards we stopped in at the Senate Bar for a few drinks. The evening was enjoyable for both of us.

February 12, 1978, was a day I'd rather not remember. It started out with my usual trek uptown after the mail. I usually made it a point to get the mail at 10:30 because that's when the bars opened. That way I could run into the Senate Bar or the Blue Ribbon for two or three quick drinks; if I stayed too long my mother would call up. I always kept a bottle hidden in the shop to get me through the day but I needed a couple of quick belts to get my day started.

When I got home, I went back to work upholstering a truck seat for one of Carbon County's trucks. Mother wasn't feeling well and her mood reflected that. She said that I wasn't doing enough upholstery or taking care of business, and I was spending too much time with Joanne. She started complaining that she never got to go anyplace because I had other interests. The day began on a sour note for both of us; however, I didn't realize how serious our conflicts were getting.

I kept nipping away at the bottle I had in the shop and made at least three trips uptown for a few more drinks. Each time, I'd tell Mother that I needed something for the shop but all I wanted was to get away, have a few drinks, and talk to somebody.

Joanne and I were going to the show that evening. I'd called her earlier to ask if she wanted to go out for supper with me, but she and her mother had already eaten. I'd changed clothes and was ready to go get

Joanne when Mother started in on me. I was trying to figure out some way that I could leave by six so I'd have an hour to stop off for a few drinks on the way. Mother started saying I never took her to the show but I could always find time to take Joanne. By then, I'd had enough to drink that I started losing control of my temper. I bumped into the coffee table and knocked a popcorn bowl onto the floor, breaking it; it had been my grandmother's so Mother really got upset. She threatened to call the sheriff which she'd done many times before.

I told her, "No reason to call the sheriff. It was an accident and I'm sorry. I haven't done anything that bad."

She said, "I am going to call the sheriff," and proceeded to walk into the bedroom and picked up the phone.

I said, "Now Mom, put that phone down. There is no reason to call the sheriff. All I am going to do is go to the show and that's it."

She said, "I am going to call him anyway."

I went into the bedroom then and said, "Mom, now put down that phone!" The last thing I remember is reaching for it

CHAPTER 19

On Trial For Murder

I was taken to the Carbon County Jail then transferred to the Yellowstone County Jail in Billings, Montana. I tried to take my own life and they decided they'd better put me where I could be under constant surveillance, or I would eventually succeed; because the Carbon County Jail was not designed so the police could keep a close watch on their prisoners.

The following court proceedings are from the transcripts of my trial which was held in the Carbon County Courthouse, Red Lodge, Montana. The transcripts contain six-hundred and twenty-four pages so I had the author condense the proceedings as much as possible.

A pre-trial hearing was held July 25, 1978. Testimony from the three psychologists who examined me was heard in order to determine whether or not I was mentally competent to stand trial in my own defense. Although their feelings were mixed about my mental competence the night of the murder, they did feel I was competent when they examined me approximately six weeks later. Since the mental incompetency plea was not allowed as a defense, my attorney relied upon a plea of self-defense.

My trial began September 11, 1978 and ended September 14, 1978. Arthur W. Ayers, Jr. was the attorney who prosecuted me, and D. Frank Kampfe was my defense attorney.

THE COURT: We will now have opening statements of Counsel, beginning with Mr. Ayers.

MR. AYERS: Thank you, Your Honor. May it please the Court, Mr. Kampfe, and Ladies and Gentlemen of the Jury. I have an opportunity at this time as attorney for the State of Montana to make a brief opening statement to tell you what the State is going to attempt to prove to you. The State's first witness will be Molly Boltz. Molly is a dispatcher with the Carbon County Sheriff's Office; the office right downstairs from here. As a dispatcher, she answers the telephone for the sheriff's department and after certain hours in the evening, for the Red Lodge Police Department. On February 12, 1978, when the Red Lodge Police Department line rang, Miss Boltz picked up the phone and heard certain goings-on which she will relate in more detail to you. She became concerned with what she heard and handed the telephone to Red Lodge Police Officer Craig Christie. Mr. Christie listened to that telephone and could hear the other end of that telephone for a period slightly in excess of thirty minutes. He made certain notes of what he heard. He will testify that what he heard caused him to believe a crime of violence was being committed. He was finally able to learn the address of the caller, 207-½ North Platte, here in Red Lodge. Thereupon, Officer Christie and Deputy Sheriff Bert J. Obert both proceeded to that location. That location is slightly more than three- hundred feet from where you are sitting right now; right down this alley at 207-½ North Platte, is a house that was occupied by the defendant, Edwin Grant Hamilton, and his mother, Mabel Johnson. Mr. Obert knocked on the door and Mr. Hamilton came to the door. Mr. Obert went in followed shortly by Mr. Christie. They discovered Mrs. Johnson in her bedroom prone with no signs of life. Subsequently, Dr. Dale Kemmerer, a physician here in RedLodge, was called; he determined for a fact that Mrs. Johnson was deceased. During this time, Sheriff Eichler arrived and arrested the defendant. Sheriff Eichler, in an attempt to learn the cause of death, ordered an autopsy whereby, Mrs. Johnson's body was transported to Great Falls, Montana. Dr. John Pfaff, a forensic pathologist, will testify as to the cause of death; he will state that in his opinion it was manual strangulation. In presenting those witnesses and perhaps a few more, the State will hope to prove to you beyond a reasonable doubt that the defendant is guilty of the crime he is charged with; deliberate homicide of Mabel Johnson on February 12, 1978. Thank You.

THE COURT: Mr. Kampfe, you may give your opening statement now.

MR. KAMPFE: Ladies and Gentlemen of the Jury, you are now full-fledged jury members. The testimony and evidence I am about to give will give you some idea of what to expect so you are able to follow the testimony. It is not my intention to mislead you. I believe that the evidence in this case will show that Grant Hamilton has spent most of his life in prison, but that at no time has he ever committed a violent act. Each and every time he found himself in trouble with the law it was a result of his sickness, commonly known as alcoholism, a sickness he has had his entire life. There will be evidence that he has attempted to seek cures for that disease. At times the cures and treatment were successful, and at other times they were unsuccessful. The evidence will show that Grant Hamilton had a very complicated, strange and involved relationship with his mother, the deceased in this matter. There will be testimony that Grant Hamilton was physically assaulted by his mother on more than one occasion, and that never in his lifetime did he lift a finger to resist that physical assault upon his being. That those physical assaults took place over a long period of time, some twenty to thirty years, and they became a part of the psychological relationship between the defendant and his mother. The testimony will show that on the night in question, February 12, 1978, Grant Hamilton's blood alcohol content was .19. There will be testimony that on the night in question, Grant was struck in the head by a telephone receiver held by his mother; that it was the first time his mother, who had previously assaulted him, ever struck him with a foreign object; in this case a telephone receiver. There will be testimony that Grant Hamilton is legally blind without his glasses; that during the struggling and fighting which occurred between him and his mother, his glasses were removed from his face as a result of a blow to the head from his mother. I anticipate there will be testimony that psychologically speaking, a person who wore glasses from the time they were six, and who is legally blind without them could have many tremendous, powerful, and overwhelming fears. The testimony from both sides will attempt to demonstrate what actually occurred on February 12, 1978. There will be testimony that this man, Grant Hamilton, was placed in reasonable fear for his life and well-being. As a part of that reasonable fear was the fact that he was legally blind without his glasses, and was overcome by fear and panic after suffering alcoholism and having been drinking the better part of the day. There will be considerable testimony of psychological assaults upon the being of Grant Hamilton for a period of twenty to thirty years, and what that does to a person; what builds up in a person's mind as a result of those psychological assaults. There will be testimony of blackouts, a common phenomenon for those afflicted with alcoholism. They do not understand or remember what happened the night before which results from overuse and abuse of intoxicating beverages. There will be testimony that alcoholism is a disease. It's an affliction whereby drinking becomes an involuntary act. Photographs will be introduced into evidence showing you, the jury, lacerations and bruises upon the face of the defendant, Grant Hamilton. These photographs were taken immediately after his arrest at approximately 7 o'clock in the evening, February 12, 1978. Grant Hamilton will be unable to tell you exactly everything that occurred. His testimony will be that after a given point, he remembers nothing. There will be testimony that Grant Hamilton gave every dime he earned to his mother and was placed in a position where he had to literally beg for spending money. There will be testimony that Mr. Hamilton's mother, would not help him with his alcoholism, but would contribute to it. And last, there will be testimony that Grant Hamilton acted as a reasonable person in self-defense under a given set of circumstances. Thank you, very much.

THE COURT: Mr. Ayers, your first witness.

MR. AYERS: Your honor, the State will call Molly Boltz.

Q. Where you employed on February 12, 1978, as a dispatcher for the Carbon County Sheriff's Department?

A. Yes, I was.

Q. Directing your attention to that evening, do you recall receiving a telephone call at approximately 6:26P.M.?

A. Yes, I do.

Q. Miss Boltz, would you describe to the Judge and to the jury what happened?

A. Okay. I answered the telephone and there was no answer. I said,

"This is the Red Lodge Police Department." I could hear arguing in the background, and to me it sounded like a couple of drunks. Craig Christie was standing nearby so I told him that it sounded like we had a fight. He'd started for the door when I heard one sentence distinctly, "You tried to call the goddamn cops on me," I told Craig, "You wait a minute and listen to this," so he took the phone.

Q. Do you have any recollection of how long he held the phone?

A. Anywhere from a half hour to forty-five minutes, somewhere in there. I don't remember.

Q. Were you doing anything during this time?

A. Oh, yes. I called the sheriff and Deputy Bert Obert and I tried to call the chief of police, but he wasn't at home. Then I called the telephone office.

Q. What was the purpose of trying to call the telephone office?

A. We were trying to trace the line to find the telephone number and address of the caller.

Q. What did Officer Christie do when he laid down the receiver or whatever it was, he did when he was finished listening?

A. He gave me the phone and told me to keep on the line. He took off and then I listened to the phone again.

Q. Did you hear anything at that time?

A. Yes, the individual on the other end was asking for help. He said his mother needed help because she'd had a heart attack. I advised him that help was on the way.

Q. Anything else that you heard?

A. He asked for his cousin or aunt and gave me the telephone number but no names.

CROSS-EX AMINATION OF MOLLY BOLTZ BY MR. KAMPFE:

Q. Now, is that what you believe there were, two drunks fighting?

A. Well, yes. It sounded like it to me.

Q. How did you arrive at the conclusion that there were two people?

A. Just by the different tones of voice; the two different voices.

Q. Would you describe the two different voices as you remember them?

A. One was deeper than the other and one was a little bit shrill, but it was indistinct; it wasn't very clear.

DIRECT EXAMINATION OF CRAIG W. CHRISTIE BY MR. AYERS:

Q. Would you describe to the Court and jury what you initially heard when you listened to the telephone?

A. I could hear what sounded like a struggle between a male and female at the other end.

Q. Could you explain why you thought there was a struggle and that there was a male and female involved?

A. I heard scuffling at the other end of the line. I heard a female voice calling for help. I inquired as to what the address was and heard what sounded like 307.

Q. Could you tell whether it was a male or female voice that gave you those numbers?

A. That was a female voice that stated those numbers on the other end of the telephone line.

Q. Was there anything else from the female voice?

A. The female voice then became muffled and unintelligible. I couldn't understand what she was trying to say.

Q. And what did you do after you thought you heard this 307?

A. I advised Miss Boltz to look in the telephone book and find all the telephone numbers of all the addresses of 307.

Q. Did you continue listening to the telephone?

A. Yes, I did.

Q. And what else, if anything, did you hear?

A. I then heard what sounded like a female subject being strangled. I could hear gasping for air and gagging and it sounded to me as if someone was being strangled at the other end of the line.

Q. And what else did you do other than listen to the telephone?

A. At that time I began to write down what I heard over the line; every word or sentence that I could make out I wrote down on a piece of paper.

Q. Officer Christie, I see that you have some notes in front of you.

Could you tell us what those are?

A. The words that I wrote down, and they are exactly as I heard them over the phone starting at 6:34 in the evening. The first thing that I wrote down was, "Goddamn it, die." This was said in a tone of voice that I would describe as being a hateful type tone of voice. And then I heard, "I am going to hell," as if the person was saying it to another person.

Then I heard, "Mama, I am sorry." That was what I would describe as an apologetic tone of voice. Then I heard, "You all right, Mama, huh?" That was a questioning type tone of voice. Then I heard, "No, no, no, Mama."

That was what I would describe as someone saying it was sorry. Then I heard, "Mama, Mama, Mama." Kind of again a questioning tone of voice.

And then I heard, "Like hell I am." That was what I would describe as a defiant tone of voice. And then I heard, "I have never done this before in my life," as if he were telling someone else. Then I heard, "I have got to find my glasses." Again, as if he were talking to someone else. And then, "Mama, Mama," again a questioning type tone of voice. And then, "Goddamn it, die," as if he were commanding or ordering. Then, "Are you going to die or not?" in a questioning but hateful tone of voice. "Die damn it," again a command type of voice where he is ordering someone. And then, "I am going to hell." Kind of again as if he were talking to someone else. And finally, "Mama," in a questioning voice.

Q. Did you hear anything further other than what you have just related to the Court and jury?

A. Yes, I did. I then heard what sounded like a call trying to be made out, oh, like someone dialing the telephone on the other end. I continued to listen and heard this same male voice say, "Hang the goddamn phone up. I have to call my cousin. My mother is dead. She had a heart attack."

Q. Did you say anything?

A. Yes, I did. I then asked the person at the other end of the line what his name was.

Q. Did you get any response and what was it?

A. Yes, the response was a male caller yelling into the telephone,

"Grant Hamilton!" At that time, I asked what his address was and he said,

"Hang up the phone. I have to call my cousin." Again, I asked him what his address was and he yelled into the phone, "207-½ North Platte!"

Q. What did you do then, Officer?

A. I advised Miss Boltz of the address and left for that address.

Q. Mr. Christie, for the benefit of the Court, would you briefly describe the house in question at 207 - ½ North Platte?

A. It is a small, wooden framed structure. It's got a brown tar paper assimilated wood covering on the outside. It's got a small entryway located on the southwest corner. From the entryway, you enter the living room. On the east side of the living room there is a bedroom with acordian type doors that draw to the center from either side. As you pass through, continuing north, you enter a dining room and to the east of the dining room is a kitchen. Northeast of the kitchen is a bathroom. Continuing north through the residence another doorway leads to the shop-laundry room and work area. Just east of the work area is another small bedroom.

Q. Was anyone else other than you and Deputy Obert at the residence?

A. Yes, Sheriff Eichler.

Q. At the time you went to the residence, where was the defendant?

A. The defendant was in the front room area just outside the bedroom door.

Q. Where was Mrs. Johnson?

A. Mrs. Johnson was lying face down on the floor approximately two feet inside the bedroom door.

Q. Did you do anything in particular regarding the decedent herself?

A. Yes, I did. I made a preliminary examination for any vital signs of life and there weren't any.

Q. Did you notice anything unusual about the telephone?

A. It was out of its cradle and I noticed that there was a small red spot on the receiver portion of the telephone that appeared to be blood.

Q. Did Sheriff Eichler do anything after he arrived at the residence?

A. Yes. I advised him of what had occurred during the telephone conversation and what we had found when we arrived at the residence. At that time Sheriff Eichler placed the defendant, Grant Hamilton, under arrest and they left the residence.

Q. Did anyone else arrive after Sheriff Eichler?

A. Yes. Dr. Kemmerer was notified and he arrived at the house to conduct an investigation of Mrs. Johnson.

Q. Could you describe to the Court and jury how the female was clothed?

A. She was clothed in a pair of what I would describe as dark green pants and a red, black, and white horizontally-striped shirt. I noticed the shirt she was wearing was inside out; the label at the back of the neck was hanging out.

Q. Can you identify this photograph?

A. That is a photograph of the victim, Mrs. Mabel Johnson, prior to any movement by anyone; as she was found at the scene.

CROSS EXAMINATION OF CRAIG W. CHRISTIE BY MR. KAMPFE:

Q. Are you familiar with the fact that Dispatcher Boltz indicated that two drunks were fighting?

A. That is correct.

Q. Now, at any time did you get the impression that there were two drunks fighting?

A. No, I did not.

Q. I believe you used the words struggle as opposed to fighting?

A. Correct.

Q. Now, how would you describe a struggle?

A. I would describe a struggle as more of a wrestling type activity rather than a fighting type activity.

Q. You did indicate that there was a male voice that was thick and slurred, did you not?

A. Yes, I did.

Q. Would that indicate to you as an officer the use and possible overuse of intoxicating beverages?

A. It would indicate to me the possible use of an intoxicating beverage or someone that was under the influence of some type of drug.

Q. And would you then put in your report that the male voice seemed to be thick and slurred; did you believe that that person was intoxicated in some manner?

A. I believed that he was under some degree of influence of an alcoholic beverage.

Q. Now, Officer Christie, during the course of your investigation on February 12, 1978, did you have occasion to have some additional photographs taken?

A. Yes, I did.

Q. And were some of those photographs taken of Grant Hamilton, the defendant in this matter?

A. Yes, they were.

Q. Now, do you know when they were taken?

A. They were taken at the sheriff's office shortly after the defendant, Mr. Hamilton, was taken into custody by the sheriff.

Q. And you observed Mr. Hamilton's face at the time that you entered the residence at approximately 7:00 o'clock on February 12, 1978, is that correct?

A. Yes, it is.

Q. Now, did Mr. Hamilton have a laceration on the left temple of his forehead?

A. Yes, he did.

Q. And was there blood around that particular area?

A. Yes, there was.

Q. Did you examine the laceration?

A. Yes, I did.

Q. And what was your conclusion?

A. My conclusion at that time was the laceration was consistent with a scratch; that it was not deep and that it did not require immediate medical attention.

Q. You utilized the phrase "scratch"; could it possibly have been caused from a blow by some object to the temple area?

A. No, because there was a tearing of the skin. And it was a surface type tear of the skin rather than a striking type wound.

Q. Is it your testimony that a blow cannot cause a tearing of the skin?

A. No, it's not my testimony that a blow cannot cause a tearing of the skin?

Q. Then a blow can cause, in your opinion, a tearing of the skin; is that correct?

A. Yes, it can.

Q. And I take it there was quite a bit of blood in that area when you first observed Mr. Hamilton?

A. There was one drip, if you will, of blood approximately three inches long?

Q. Now, did Mr. Hamilton have other possible cuts or bruises on his facial area that you observed?

A. Yes, he did.

Q. And were there more than one?

A. Yes, there were.

Q. And in fact did that have some discoloration at any time that you might have observed it?

A. Yes, it did.

Q. And was that possibly a light yellow with maybe a tint of green in it?

A. Yes, it was.

Q. Now, when you first observed Mr. Hamilton at the residence on February 12, 1978, was he wearing his eyeglasses?

A. No, he was not.

Q. At any time in your presence did Mr. Hamilton make any reference to the fact that he was not wearing eyeglasses?

A. Yes, he did.

Q. And if you recall, what did he indicate?

A. I believe that on at least two occasions he requested his glasses.

Q. Did you at any time find a broken popcorn bowl?

A. Yes, I did.

Q. And in what room did you locate that?

A. That was located in the dining room just north of the living room.

Mr. Kampfe: I have nothing further.

THE COURT: Witness excused.

DIRECT EXAMINATION OF DALE L. KEMMERER, M.D. BY MR. AYERS:

Q. Dr. Kemmerer, were you contacted on the evening of February 12, 1978 concerning an apparent death?

A. Yes, I was.

Q. And where did you go?

A. The sheriff called me and asked me to go the residence behind the courthouse here.

Q. Is it behind the courthouse or the courthouse annex?

A. Behind the courthouse annex and the welfare office. I went there and saw Officer Christie and Bert Obert and there was a woman who was dead on the floor.

Q. What did you do in examining her?

A. Well, the usual things; looking at her pupils and checking to see if she had a pulse or any respirations. There were no signs of life and I pronounced her dead.

Q. Did you notice anything about that person other than what you have already described?

A. Yes.

Q. Would you tell us what that is please?

A. My attention was called to the fact that there was some blood on her face and in her nose, and over the ridge of her nose there was a bruise. I marked on my notes that she had a necromantic spot and at least six puncture wounds or small cuts on the right neck. She was also wet under her pelvis indicating that she had passed some urine. I thought that she had recently died and made my observations known to the police officers that were there.

CROSS EXAMINATION OF DALE L. KEMMERER M.D. BY MR. KAMPFE:

Q. Did you have occasion to examine Mr. Hamilton? A. Yes, I did.

Q. Are you familiar with the uncorrected eyesight of 200/400? A. Yes.

Q. And am I correct that that would qualify someone with that eyesight as being blind?

A. Yes.

Q. Did it appear that it was bothering Mr. Hamilton because he did not have his glasses on his face?

A. Yes.

Q. Now, did you observe any bruises on Mr. Hamilton?

A. Yes.

Q. Can a blow to the head by a physical object cause a bruise?

A. Yes.

Q. When you observed Mr. Hamilton at the Carbon County Sheriff's Office did you detect any indication of drinking or the consumption of alcohol beverages by Mr. Hamilton?

A. I suspected that was a possibility.

Cross Examination of Sheriff James F. Eichler by Mr. Kampfe brought forth the following information: Taken from the Hamilton-Johnson residence were liquor containers and some liquor; half a fifth of Calvert's whiskey, a Spanada wine bottle, two full Old Milwaukee beer cans, a cardboard carton of Magill whiskey, an empty Calverts bottle, one full fifth of French Grenadine, two empty pints of Calverts, and four empty Milwaukee beer cans.

DIRECT EXAMINATION OF JOHN PFAFF, JR. M.D. BY MR. AYERS:

Q. Are you consulting pathologist to the Carbon County Memorial Hospital here in Red Lodge?

A. Yes.

Q. Would you describe the body as you first examined it?

A. The body was fully clothed and the hands and face were covered with plastic sacks, as is the usual procedure. The clothing was removed and the body appeared to be that of a well-developed, well nourished, and aged white female. In measuring it, we found it to be 4'10½" in height, and it weighed 94 pounds.

Q. Could you tell us about your internal examination of the body?

A. In the head there was no evidence of fracture to any bone; and there was no evidence of hemorrhage or other injury to the brain. In the chest and abdomen there was also no evidence of bony fracture or evidence of trauma, that is physical impact to any organ in the body. In the neck area there was hemorrhage beneath the bruise on the left side of the neck.

There were multiple areas of hemorrhage within the muscles of the neck structure about the voice box, which we call the larynx. In addition, a bone present in the upper part of the neck, which is located at the base of the tongue, had a fracture injury. It had been broken and there was bleeding about the fracture sight.

Q. Are you able to state the cause of death with a reasonable degree of medical certainty?

A. Yes.

Q. What was the cause of death of Mabel Johnson?

A. Manual strangulation.

Q. What is your opinion as to the general health of Mabel Johnson prior to her death?

A. Excellent for her age.

Q. Do you have any opinion as to how long it would take to effectively manually strangle a person of Mrs. Johnson's age, weight, health, and height under ideal conditions; when I say ideal conditions I am talking about without resistance?

A. For complete cessation of all vital functions and if one assumes complete airway constriction or occlusion, and complete occlusion of all blood vessels leading from the heart to the brain, then it wouldn't take longer than two or three minutes. If the heart were affected by lack of oxygen, it would take a much shorter time; but, Mrs. Johnson had very little hardening of the arteries and no evidence of heart disease. Because of that, I think the most likely time would be two or three minutes. It could of course, be considerably longer than this if the pressure had been applied intermittently.

Q. Would it have been longer if the victim would have struggled and in fact fought her assailant?

A. With struggle one usually assumes some intermittency of pressure so this would tend to delay it.

DIRECT EXAMINATION OF BENJAMIN J. KARAS, M.D. BY DR. KAMPFE:

Q. Dr. Karas, what is your occupation?

A. Physician and surgeon.

Q. Are you a general practitioner here in Red Lodge?

A. Yes, I am.

Q. Doctor, in the last several years have you had occasion to see a patient by the name of Mabel Johnson?

A. Yes, I have.

Q. And directing your attention to 1976, did you have the occasion to see her that year?

A. Yes, I did.

Q. Would you describe the significant occasion in which you saw her professionally?

A. Yes. To give just a little background, she had been treated by myself for an acute duodenal ulcer with several types of medication. During May of 1976, she was brought to the hospital after an apparent suicide attempt. She described a number of things that were going on that were rather chaotic to her and she apparently took what pills she had left. We didn't know exactly how many she took at that time, but she was brought in groggy and we treated her conservatively and she did improve.

Q. Now, you indicated that she described some of the events that had been happening to her. Were there any of those that stood out in your mind?

A. A couple that she mentioned. One was difficulty with her son who had lost his job at that time. Another was her television had just gone out and she mentioned this as a thing that really seemed to bother her.

Q. And as a result of that did you form an opinion as to her psychological condition?

A. I think at that time she had acute depressive reaction, and had made this rather abortive suicide attempt.

Q. Did you form an opinion as to whether or not she had any symptoms of neurosis?

A. I think one of the precipitating things in this event indicated neurosis. People usually don't commit suicide when their television goes out.

Q. I direct your attention to February 3rd, 1978. Did you have the occasion to see Mabel Johnson at that time?

A. Yes, I gave her a prescription at that time.

Q. Is that your signature that appears in the bottom right-hand corner?

A. I would say so. It's one prescription that she didn't have filled.

Q. And how can you tell it had not been filled?

A. There is no pharmacist stamp on it and they are required by law so they can't be re-issued.

Q. Now, Doctor, what was the prescription for?

A. This is a prescription for a drug called Tranxene, which is a mild tranquilizer. At that time she'd had an injury to her chest; a dog had jumped on her and she had some sore ribs. This was given to help her rest at night.

Q. How would she react if she was not taking the prescribed tranquilizer?

A. At that time she probably would have more restlessness and pain. She probably would be irritable; she would be more anxious, certainly. She was a patient incidentally who was rather erratic about taking her medications. She would take one of a particular medicine when she felt like it and on the other hand, she would take more than she needed to take at the time.

Q. Would that erratic pattern fit in with her basic personality as you observed her?

A. I think so.

CROSS-EXAMINATION OF DR. BENJAMIN KARAS BY MR. AYERS:

Dr. Karas, would her failure to have that prescription filled and take the medication prescribed cause Mrs. Johnson to become violent or maybe violently aggressive?

A. I think it's a relative thing. I think she would be more aggressive if she didn't take it.

Q. This prescription is basically to ease pain caused by the dog jumping on her; is that correct?

A. That's right.

Mr. Ayers: I have nothing further.

THE COURT: Witness excused.

DIRECT EXAMINATION OF DR. NED TRANEL BY MR. KAMPFE

Q. Doctor, what is your background in the area of clinical psychology?

A. I have been practicing psychology for about eighteen years. I first worked as a professor at the University of South Dakota. After that I worked as a research psychologist in the Veterans Administration. Following that I worked in the Wyoming Mental Health Center as chief psychologist. Following that I worked at the Mental Health Center in Miles City, Montana, and for the last six years I have been in private practice in Billings, Montana.

Q. Can you explain what a clinical psychologist is?

A. A clinical psychologist is a person who works with the scientific understanding of human behavior. A clinical psychologist is primarily interested in the functions of abnormal behavior. The tools that he uses are tests developed by scientific laboratories and professional groups such as neurologists, biochemists, educators, and physiologists.

Q. Now, Doctor, have you had the occasion to do some professional work with a Mr. Grant Hamilton?

A. Yes, I interviewed him on several occasions and I also conducted a complete psychological examination of Mr. Hamilton.

Q. Could you describe your findings and the tests?

A. When we assess human behavior, we are interested in three main areas. The first area we look at is that person's general intelligence. The second is the person's vocational interest pattern. The third is the area of personality status. I used the Wechsler Intelligence Scale, the Strong Vocational Interest Test, the Minnesota Multiphasic Personality Inventory, and then I added others; the Wechsler Memory Scale; the Graham-Kendall Memory for Designs Test, the Wide Range Achievement Test, and the Rorschach Ink Blot Test.

Q. Could you give us a description of the results of those tests?

A. Yes. The first area of assessment revealed that Mr. Hamilton was functioning at a level of intellectual development which is consistent with his chronological age. The overall IQ score traced him in the bright-normal range. There were no indications of any chronic impairments in the learning processes. He is still able to learn at a level consistent with his chronological age. His reading grade level is that of a high school graduate; about 12.2 grade equivalent. His spelling grade level is at about a seventh-grade level, and his arithmetic grade level is about a sixth- grade level. Regarding his vocational interests, he has no fixed or specific occupational commitments. He has a rather low level of achievement as far as his vocational aspirations. He is a man that would be content with a fairly average or even mediocre level of vocational direction. The most extensive area of the examination revealed that he is experiencing a severe personality disorder characterized technically as a condition of schizophrenic reaction (chronic undifferentiated type) and that is accompanied by features of pathological intoxication.

Mr. Ayers: Excuse me, Dr. Tranel. Your Honor, Dr. Tranel is now testifying to things which I believe are out of the scope of the issues presented in this case.

The Court: On that point I would like to see Counsel in Chambers.

Court will remain in session; the jury will remain at ease.

The Judge, Prosecuting Attorney, and the Defense Attorney then meet in the Judge's Chambers:

The Court: What's your position on this, Frank?

Frank Kampfe: Dr. Tranel's testimony has nothing to do with mental disease or defect. His testimony is directed towards the key issue in this case and that is the state of mind of the defendant on the night in question, and based upon his scientific tests and evaluations

Mr. Ayers: Your Honor, Mr. Kampfe has previously withdrawn the defense of mental disease or defect and I think he is trying to present evidence through the backdoor. In the matters which Mr. Kampfe says that he is trying to establish through the testimony of Dr. Tranel, I submit that they are irrelevant and inappropriate to the defense of self-defense and justifiable use of force. That defense is based upon the reasonable man standard, and not the Grant Hamilton standard.

Mr. Kampfe: This man can testify as to things directed toward a particular state of mind which is ultimate in this particular case; that is, what was happening in the man's mind. That's what this jury has to resolve. Dr. Tranel's testimony is clearly relevant to those issues. I have withdrawn the mental disease or defect defense. I am not going into that. The psychological condition of the man has bearing on what was in his mind and that's what the testimony is being introduced for.

The Court: I can understand it being relevant to the state of mind, but I am wondering what state of mind has to do with the defense of self-defense.

Mr. Kampfe: The jury, based on the instructions that are going to be given, have to go through the knowing and purposeful state of mind. Dr. Tranel's testimony is going to be directed in that area. On self-defense the state of mind is whether or not he was reasonably placed in fear for his life. That's what self-defense is all about.

The Court: As Mr. Ayers says, it's not the Hamilton standard, or psychopath standard, or schizophrenic standard, or alcoholic standard; it's a reasonable person standard, isn't it?

Mr. Kampfe: Placed in those circumstances. The Court: Reasonable person.

Mr. Kampfe: And that's all the circumstances; the past relationship between the defendant and the victim. Those are the circumstances which contribute to the defense of self-defense, and contribute to his state of mind at the time in question. It's all of the circumstances put together.

The Court: Well, I think the circumstances between the victim and the defendant are certainly admisable. Their relationship, I think, is admisable but it seems to me only as it pertains to a reasonable person standard.

Mr. Kampfe: Let me go on. A man that is legally blind without his glasses has been affected psychologically. The jury has to take that into consideration. When you ask the jury to take the reasonable man standard, part of that's got to be a man that's legally blind without his glasses. It can't be John J. Citizen that doesn't have glasses, and who was placed in that circumstance, and being hit by his mother for the first time with an object.

The Court: When you get into this business of alcoholism and these things, what relevancy do those things have on self-defense?

Mr. Kampfe: We are back at what's going on in his mind.

The Court: It may be such a thing Mr. Ayers, that you can't strain the tobacco juice out of the milk here. I don't know.

Mr. Ayers: Well, Judge, I think it's apparent that Dr. Tranel is testifying only about Grant Hamilton's reactions under these circumstances.

The Court: Well--

Mr. Ayers: He is not testifying about what a reasonable man would do with this.

(Thereupon further argument was had off the record)

The Court: The reasonableness is to be determined from the viewpoint of a reasonable person in an active situation.

Mr. Kampfe: That's exactly correct, and that means the type of emotional stress the defendant had been under; the type the victim had put him under, whether the victim was the aggressor that night, and how that man would react under that kind of stress. That's the thrust of Dr.

Tranel's whole testimony.

(After further discussion, the Court and Counsel returned to the courtroom.)

CHAPTER 20

Our Sons Inherit Us*

FURTHER EXAMINATION OF DR. NED TRANEL BY MR. KAMPFE:

Q. Before the slight break, Doctor, we were discussing the psychological condition that you found in Mr. Hamilton. Would you put that in layman's terms?

A. Yes. Mr. Hamilton's personality condition is characterized by the technical label which I described as schizophrenic reaction. The features of that include extreme dependence, very low tolerance for frustration, a general reduction in coping skills or the ability to deal with problems in the world, emotional immaturity, reactions to stress with significant depression, a generalized feeling of inferiority and inadequacy, and an inability to maintain independent social roles.

Q. Now, based upon your expertise, is there any patterns for the causes of that type of personality?

A. Yes, there are a number of causes. In Mr. Hamilton's case, we found that the major contributing factor was a pathologically symbiotic relationship with his mother. A symbiotic relationship is one in which there is mutual dependence. One is unable to maintain an existence without the other. It was not a healthy interdependence such as might be found in a marriage relationship, but a pathological or unhealthy dependence in which one could not exist with his emotional or psychological integrity without the other. I say that because with that feature of chronic undifferentiated schizophrenia, the major cause is what we call a schizophrenogenic parent.

118

Q. Could you explain a schizophrenogenic parent?

A. Yes. That's a parent which contributes to the formation of a schizophrenic condition by way of the child. In this case we are talking about an adult, but there is a long history to this. The way the parent treats the child means it's generating, therefore the last part of the word, schizophrenogenic. I could elaborate on the features of a schizophrenogenic parent if I have not made that clear.

Q. If you would please.

A. We had to reconstruct Mr. Hamilton's life history and his present symptom pattern in order to determine the characteristics of his mother. Based on his life history and his relationship with his mother, and his present symptom pattern we were then able to determine the schizophrenogenic features in the parent which contributed to this condition. Those features are, first of all, a person who is dominating and cold. The coldness refers to kind of an emotional refrigeration type of situation, where the person doesn't distinguish correctly between success and failure experiences. Both success and failure are reacted to with similar emotional responses. The next feature of a schizophrenogenic parent is excessive overprotectiveness, which often continues far beyond the need of a child for protection. The next feature is one which has been described extensively in literature by a researcher at Louisiana State named Bateson; it is called a double bind characteristic. A double bind characteristic in a schizophrenogenic parent is one in which the person sends conflicting messages; behaving in one way towards a person but feeling another way, such as a parent in relatively normal circumstances who might be fatigued or tired at night.

The child asks to have a story read and the mother grudgingly says yes, I will read you the story; but she holds the child on her lap while all the time, she is being quite rejecting because of her exhaustion. The child gets a love response by the behavior of holding but another response by the emotional feeling of the mother. Another way of describing that might be to say a double bind parent will encourage independence verbally but foster dependence by the way the child is treated. So, the child might be rated for not achieving independence but as soon as he has achieved some independence or attempts to, he is severely criticized, and what he is doing is wrong. The messages are inconsistent and the child is placed in what is sometimes called a no-win condition; no matter what he does, it can't be right. I elaborated on that somewhat because it's one of the major features of a schizophrenogenic parent.

Q. Doctor, would another example be a parent who would accost a son for being an alcoholic and then turn around and buy him booze?

A. That would be a dramatic example of it, yes. Another example of a schizophrenogenic parent is one who usually has a rigid and moralistic view; in the negative sense of that term, toward sexual adjustment. This is usually manifested by again encouraging appropriate sexual roles in the child verbally but then rejecting the child whenever he shows an indication of having achieved sexual maturity and independence.

Q. Would that be, say, a parent who encourages a marriage but at the same time tries to break up the marriage?

A. Yes, for example, encourage the child by saying why don't you get married; you are old enough to get married; when are you going to get married? But when a prospective marriage mate is suggested then that is met with disapproval. There is another aspect to the schizophrenogenic parent and that is the smothering feature; the parent keeps the child dependent by making some of the major decisions in life for him, and then criticizes him for his own independent decision making. As an example, the parent would manage the person's finances or criticize the way he is investing his money.

Q. Would you please go on with Mr. Hamilton's condition as you found him?

A. I was interested in the presence of any distortion or disruption in his learning processes. His ability to learn when he is not under the influence of alcohol is intact. I noted that he was under a chronic and continual form of severe stress. The stress that he was under was caused by the schizophrenogenic parent and this was accompanied by a continual assault on the integrity of his personality functioning. His ability to cope with the stress that he was under was eroded over a long period of time. Stress has a cumulative effect and it built up to a point where we noted in the test that his level of ego strength (ego strength is a term which describes general coping skill or problem-solving ability) was about two standard deviations below average or normal. Two standard deviations would mean that that would occur very infrequently and is found only among people who have lost the ability to tolerate stress. It has reached almost a zero point. That was significant because it was in sharp contrast to his general emotional makeup. Most of the measures on his tests were two standard deviations above average while his general coping skill was about two standard deviations below average. To answer your question more specifically, the stress that he was under would be characterized by the third stage of stress which is the stage of exhaustion. This stage of exhaustion of decompensation occurs when one's store of coping skills or problem-solving abilities is completely exhausted.

Q. Would verbal assaults or verbal put-downs create a stress that you have described?

A. Well, that would be one form of stress. The other form of stress was the general summary of the schizophrenogenic conditions of the mother, and so the way he was treated subjected him to a chronic stress pattern. He perceived threat in that stress pattern and he attempted to cope by extricating himself; by getting himself out of that stress pattern. He repeatedly made attempts to do that, but because of this symbiotic relationship with his mother he would have to return to her and look to her for sources of comfort and support.

Q. Would physical slapping of the face create that type of stress? A. Yes. Of course, that would be a direct assault upon his person.

Q. In Mr. Hamilton's case where he has very poor eyesight, does that become more of an issue than for someone who has normal eyesight with glasses?

A. Well, yes. We see it in some of the work I do with senile patients in a nursing home. For example, if a person loses his glasses, for you that might be a minor inconvenience, but for them it can be an extremely stressful experience. A strong fear reaction sets in because the stress or threat to one's existence is quite severe of course.

Q. Is fear and panic one of the natural results from someone who might have a perceptual disorder as a result of losing their glasses, if they have very poor eyesight?

A. Yes, fear and panic are the first reactions to a perceptual distortion. It was nicely described by Admiral Byrd who had a white-out in the Antarctic; panic and fear set in immediately because he knew that he couldn't cope and stay alive unless that perceptual distortion was somehow corrected.

Q. If Grant Hamilton had been verbally accosted by his mother, and his mother then threatened to have him put in jail, and then Mr. Hamilton was struck by a telephone in the head, could he have been placed in reasonable fear of imminent danger?

A. Oh, yes.

Q. Could he have reasonably believed that it was either he or the aggressor at that time?

A. Oh, yes.

Mr. Kampfe: No further questions. You may examine.

CROSS-EXAMINATION OF DR. NED TRANEL BY MR. AYERS:

Q. Could you tell me, Doctor, on May 30th, 1978, approximately how long you spent interviewing Mr. Hamilton?

A. Yes, I can. The examination continued for approximately five hours. Part of that time included my interview with him and part of that time, he completed some tests on his own.

Q. Your actual time with him before that interview was about two hours, wasn't it?

A. When I was with him directly myself, yes.

Q. And when was the next time that you interviewed Mr. Hamilton or tested him?

A. The second examination was dated September 1st, 1978.

Q. Less than two weeks ago?

A. Yes.

Q. How long did that test take?

A. An hour and fifteen minutes.

Q. All of the opinions you have testified to here today result from tests or your interviews with Mr. Hamilton?

A. Yes, that is correct.

Q. Absent the relationship between Grant Hamilton and his mother, and it's your opinion, is it not, that Mr. Hamilton is not to be considered a dangerous person?

A. My report indicated that Mr. Hamilton had a pathologically symbiotic relationship with his mother, and that any hostility was narrowly circumscribed. He was not a generally dangerous person.

Q. Mabel Johnson is no longer with us so that violence, or the potential for violence, is no longer present?

A. That's correct.

Q. And he is safe enough to be out on the street right now?

A. That's my opinion.

Mr. Ayers: Nothing further.

DIRECT EXAMINATION OF GARY BOUNOUS BY MR. KAMPFE:

Q. What is your present occupation?

A. I am a psychiatric social worker.

Q. Mr. Bounous, what is your educational background?

A. A Bachelor's Degree from the University of Minnesota. I attended graduate school at the University of Minnesota and received a Master's Degree in Psychiatric Social Work from that university in June of 1967.

Q. What has been your work background based upon these degrees?

A. I spent three years at the Veteran's Neuropsychiatric Hospital in Sheridan, Wyoming. During that time, I probably saw 1500 or 2000 cases of alcoholism in a hospital setting. Following that, I went to work for a comprehensive health care center in Oregon. I spent 20 to 30 percent of my time dealing with alcoholism in individuals or families. I was a consultant for the Rimrock Guidance Foundation, here in Billings, which is an alcohol treatment agency. For five years I was a full-time employee of the South-Central Montana Regional Mental Health Center. I have remained a part time employee of the Mental Health Center and I'm also in private practice.

Q. Could you tell the jury what alcoholism is?

A. Alcoholism, in my opinion, is a disease characterized by the episodic, habitual, and/or addictive use of alcohol. When it interferes with one's health, employment, relationship with other people, and one's behavior in general.

Q. Would you agree or disagree that alcoholism is a disease?

A. I would agree. The American Medical Association recognized it as such in 1957. The American Psychiatric Association also recognizes alcoholism as a disease.

Q. Is there such a thing as alcoholic blackout?

A. Yes.

Q. Would you describe what that means?

A. Alcoholic blackout or pathological intoxication is a condition that occurs when alcohol depresses the higher functions of the brain. Alcohol is a depressant. The cortical function of the brain is memory; give the unknown amount of alcohol and depending upon the individual, the circumstances and emotions, they have no memory for what happens during the time that they drink, or they only have partial memory. Somebody that has had an alcoholic blackout could theoretically say, "I was drinking and I woke up the next day and didn't have any memory of where my car was."

Q. As you have described alcoholic amnesia or blackout, is that a common phenomenon that occurs with alcoholism?

A. Yes, when determining whether someone is having an alcohol problem, one of the things to look for is periods of memory loss that's reported by the patient, or other people who have been with or have seen the patient.

Q. Could you explain the significance of a 1.9 tenths of 1 percent blood alcohol content?

A. I would say somebody who had a blood alcohol content of .19 percent was very seriously intoxicated. .05% which is less than a third of that, is a level at which the higher cortical functions are affected. I mean things like judgement, reason, impulse control, and frustration tolerance. Somebody with a blood alcohol content of .19 % would be seriously impaired in those areas. Loss of what's generally known as psychomotor coordination begins to go at 1/10 of 1 percent. A coma, which is towards the other end of the extreme, is understood to occur at about .40 % . Death from the consumption of alcohol typically occurs at somewhere between .60% and .70%

Q. Am I correct in assuming that one's judgement would be seriously impaired at .19%?

A. You are correct in assuming that judgement would start to be impaired in a noticeable way at .05%, but by the time you get to .19% I guess you can multiply that by three and one-half.

Mr. Kampfe: I have nothing further.

Q. How long have you lived in Red Lodge?

A. Well, for a good number of years.

Q. During those years have you had an opportunity to become acquainted with the defendant, Grant Hamilton?

A. For six months of last year, yes.

Q. Did you also have an opportunity to become acquainted with Mabel Johnson, his mother?

A. At that time. Before that I didn't know her well.

Q. During those six months did you get to know Grant fairly well?

A. Oh, yes.

Q. Would you say that you were dating one another?

A. Yes.

Q. And as that relationship progressed, did you have any plans for the future?

A. Yes, we were going to be married in April.

Q. Did you have an opportunity to observe both Grant and his mother?

A. Not often, but a few times.

Q. What did she think about yourself and Grant's relationship?

A. Well, I believe she was jealous. She did not want us to get married.

Q. Can you cite the reasons why you concluded that she was jealous?

A. She would say to me that we won't be married, and things like that. I could tell by her actions that she didn't want us to be married.

Q. Did you and Grant ever go somewhere together that made her angry?

A. I believe we took a trip to Cooke City, It didn't make her angry but she wasn't too happy that we went up there.

Q. Why?

A. Because, I believe Grant and his mother had a chance to go up there to Cooke City the next day, Sunday.

Q. And because you went with him, she was unable to go?

A. Right.

Q. Did you ever go shopping or take a drive to Billings or somewhere else?

A. Yes.

Q. When you did that, whose vehicle did you take?

A. Grant's truck.

Q. And who drove?

A. Grant did.

Q. When you went to Billings who usually sat next to Grant?

A. Well, on a couple of instances there Mabel did.

Q. She would sit between the two of you?

A. Yes.

Q. What did he tell you about his mother's feelings toward you?

A. Oh, he always told me that she loved me and that she cared a great deal for me. He wanted me to know that she cared for me, you know.

Q. Well, did you believe it?

A. Well, I let him think that I did. Miss Johnson: No further questions.

CROSS-EX AMINATION OF JOANNE LAHTI BY MR. AYERS:

Q. Miss Lahti, would you think that it would be accurate to describe the relationship, except for February 12, 1978, between Mr. Hamilton and his mother as being close?

A. I believe it would be, yes.

Q. And how would you describe Mrs. Johnson prior to her death in terms of neatness in her own attire?

A. She was always a neat woman. She was very clean.

Q. Was she fussy about the way she looked?

A. Yes, she always liked to look nice and she did.

Q. Could you even describe it to the point of being vain?

A. Could be.

Q. And fussy about her hair?

A. Yes.

Q. About the way, which kind of clothes she had on and how they looked?

A. Well, she liked to look nice as far as I know.

Q. And the times you were at the house, were you able to get an opinion as to whether that house was dirty, messed up, or neat?

A. It looked neat.

Q. Did Mrs. Johnson ever express concern to you about Mr. Hamilton's drinking?

A. She would say occasionally that he would drink a little too much.

Q. And did she ever say anything to you about her concern about his heavy drinking?

A. Not a lot. I couldn't say a lot.

Q. Did she ever mention that he drank?

A. Yes, and she didn't like that.

Q. She didn't like his heavy drinking but she didn't object if he just went out and had a couple of drinks?

A. Not to my knowledge, no.

Q. Did you ever on occasion go out and have a few drinks with her?

A. A couple of times, on Saturday nights, we would go out, and just have a couple of beers, then we would come home. Grant would always be the one to suggest coming home first.

Q. But she did voice objection on occasions if he would go out and actually get drunk; isn't that correct?

A. Yes.

Q. Do you recall talking to Mr. Hamilton on February 12, 1978?

A. He called me up at 4:00 in the afternoon and asked me to go out and have dinner with him, but I was eating.

Q. About how long did you talk to Mr. Hamilton?

A. Oh, I'd say about twenty minutes or a half-hour.

Q. Could you tell whether or not he'd been drinking?

A. No, I could not. He sounded like he was just fine.

Q. Sounded sober?

A. Yes, he did.

Mr. Ayers: I have nothing further, your Honor.

THE COURT: Have a seat Mr. Hamilton.

(Defendant is seated at this time.)

THE COURT: It is my duty as Judge, Mr. Hamilton, to advise you of your rights so far as testifying in your own behalf is concerned. I want to make sure that you understand that you don't have to testify unless you want to. If you don't testify, the county attorney can't comment on that to the jury; he can't indicate that that means you are guilty or anything like that. On the other hand, if you do testify, you will be put under cross- examination by the county attorney the same as any other witness. You won't have any special privileges because you are the defendant and that means if your testimony is different than other statements you have made, he may use those other statements to impeach your testimony and so forth. Do you understand?

Defendant Hamilton: Yes, sir.

The Court: I should also like to ask you if you are satisfied with the services of Mr. Kampfe?

Mr. Hamilton: More than satisfied.

The Court: You have no complaints at all?

Mr. Hamilton: No, sir. Your honor, it seems like in the past I have always hidden my record or denied it and so forth. I just think it should come out. I am tired of hiding.

The Court: Okay, that is something else that, as I understand Mr. Kampfe in his opening statement said he intends to bring out your past criminal record, and that again, is your choice. If you don't bring it out, I probably would not let the county attorney go into that.

Mr. Hamilton: The only thing I may be sketchy on, Your Honor, is dates of convictions and releases, but the rest of it should be the whole truth.

Mr. Kampfe: The defense calls to the stand, Mr. Hamilton.

Pages of the transcript contain a brief summary of Grant Hamilton's life story, which was related to the Court and the Jury by Grant Hamilton.

DIRECT EXAMINATION OF MR. HAMILTON CONTINUES BY MR. KAMPFE:

Q. Are you tired of living out of a bottle?

A. I don't ever want to see one of any kind. I am not saying that just to be saying it. I have never said it before. I have had it.

Q. Of all the crimes you testified to this afternoon, were any of those crimes of violence?

A. Never.

Q. Was alcohol connected with those?

A. I would say in every instance. In some, I got away with it.

Q. Do you remember February 12, 1978?

A. Vaguely, yes.

Q. Did your mother have a quick temper?

A. She had quite a temper.

Q. Had she ever physically accosted you prior to February 12, 1978?

A. How do you mean physically?

Q. Well, did she ever slap you around?

A. She'd get mad and she'd slap me and she would take her fist and pound on me.

Q. To your knowledge had she ever struck you with an object prior to that day?

A. No, she never had.

Q. Had she ever verbally accosted you?

A. She had, yes. If I come home drunk.

Q. Had she ever verbally accosted you and embarrassed you in front of your friends?

A. Yes, she has on occasion.

Q. I'm handing you this popcorn bowl. Do you recognize it?

A. Yes. I think that belonged to my grandmother. It wasn't expensive or anything, but it was kind of a keepsake.

Q. Do you recall anything about this popcorn bowl when this argument was going on between you and your mother?

A. I think I broke it. Now, I can't say for sure but I think I stumbled against the coffee table and broke it; and that's when, boy, that's when she blew her top at that time.

Q. What do you mean blew her top?

A. Well, she was just screaming, yelling, hollering, probably calling me about everything under the sun.

Q. Swear at you?

A. Oh, yes.

Q. Did she threaten to do anything at that time?

A. Call the sheriff, which was a standard phrase with her.

Q. What did she do after she made that threat?

A. Went into her bedroom and proceeded to call the sheriff.

Q. Do you recall if you were struck?

A. I couldn't swear one way or the other but I think it was because I reached for the phone.

Q. Did you ever think she would hit you with an object?

A. On occasion she has thrown things and this and that; maybe at me; maybe not at me; if she'd get really mad, she would throw something down.

Q. What's the next thing you remember, Grant?

A. I remember kind of groping around trying to find my glasses but I couldn't find them. And the next thing I remember is trying to pick my mother up and put her on the bed. She had had a couple of strokes before, so I was trying to put her on the bed when I turned around and looked and I seen Mr. Obert and Craig Christie. I think one of them said, "What are you trying to do?" I said, "I am trying to help my mother," and I think Mr. Obert told me to go sit down, which I did.

Q. Were you then arrested by Sheriff Eichler and taken to the jail here?

A. Yes.

Q. Did you kill your mother, Grant?

A. So help me God, I don't know. I can't...I knew it happened; I just can't believe I did. There was nobody there but us, but I just can't believe I done it. But I know it's so, and I know she's gone. I don't know. I don't know. If I did, it wasn't me.

Q. Mr. Kampfe: Your witness, Mr. Ayers.

CROSS EXAMINATION OF EDWIN GRANT HAMILTON BY MR. AYERS:

(Mr. Ayers questions Grant about his past criminal history)

Testimony continues:

Q. After seven months of reflection, you cannot recall February 12, 1978; is that correct?

A. From the 10th of February to the 12th, I really can't recall too much.

Q. So in seven months of reflection, you can't recall either?

A. In seven months all I have thought about is that day and that night. I have run it over in my mind back and forth, every way I possibly could, and I still come up with the same thing; just what I remember now.

Q. You don't recall talking to me in the Carbon County Sheriff's Office?

A. No. I probably talked to you; I probably talked to everybody, I don't know. That night I didn't even know who arrested me, or who was in the

house. I knew later on but I didn't that night. I couldn't name Mr. Obert or Mr. Christie. In fact, I didn't even know Jim arrested me; but I have known Jim Eichler for years, and if he said he arrested me, he arrested me.

Q. Do you recall telling me that you did not go uptown until afternoon; that you did not drink until afternoon?

A. I am sorry, but I just don't.

Q. Do you recall telling me that you only left the house once that day to go to Safeway to buy some beer, and then go over to the Senate and have a couple?

A. No, I don't recall telling you that.

Q. Do you recall doing that?

A. I had beer in the icebox so I assume I must have went to the

KwikStop or Safeway, or someplace and got it.

Q. Do you recall with particularly making arrangements with Miss Lahti to go to the show that night?

A. Definitely.

Q. Do you recall calling up and asking her to go out that night to have some pizza?

A. I don't remember that but I do remember that we were going to the show. I guess that wouldn't be the first time I stood her up.

Q. In response to some of Mr. Kampfe's questions; you have told the jury that your mother had a quick temper, and that as a result from time to time, she slapped you and beat up on you with her fist; is that right?

A. I wouldn't say beat up on me, no.

Q. Did she ever cause you any injury by doing that?

A. Not that I recall.

Q. You told Mr. Kampfe that you went uptown two or three times for drinks that day?

A. Well, I assume I did. I went uptown two or three times a day a lot from February 10th on. Every time I'd get a chance, I would make an excuse to get away from the house so I could go uptown and have a few quick ones.

Q. You are telling me that you don't remember; is that correct?

A. I don't think I do for sure. I must have went uptown that day because I brought a pint home, and I know that wouldn't last very long.

Q. But you don't really know whether you got it on the 12th or the 11th or the 10th, do you?

A. No, I don't know too much about the last fifteen years of my life, Mr. Ayers.

Q. Do you recall me asking on February 12, 1978, if anything had happened that day to cause you anger towards your mother, and your answer: no, I don't see that I could be?

A. There have been times I have been mad inside, but I have held it inside. I'd just leave the house and walk away.

Q. Do you recall me asking you whether your mother was mad at you that day?

A. No, I don't. I really don't. I don't recall talking to you or talking to anybody. Seemed like the main thing I was worried about my dog.

(Testimony was heard concerning the argument with Grant's mother, over her call to the police. The prosecution closed with these final statements.)

Q. How much do you weigh now, Mr. Hamilton?

A. About one-hundred-twenty pounds.

Q. How much did you weigh on February 12, 1978?

A. Probably about the same. I have never weighed over one-hundred-twenty-five.

Q. How tall are you?

A. 5'7".

Mr. Ayers: Nothing further, your Honor.

DIRECT TESTIMONY OF BARBAR A RYAN BY MISS JOHNSON, MR. KAMPFE's ASSISTANT:

Q. Mr. Ryan, how long have you lived in the RedLodge area?

A. Off and on about six years.

Q. Where do you work?

A. At the Carbon County Health Care Center.

Q. What is your occupation?

A. I am a licensed practical nurse.

Q. Ms. Ryan, in the time that you lived in RedLodge, have you become acquainted with Grant Hamilton?

A. Yes, I have. I was involved in a Christian endeavor called the Soup Shack that was located on Broadway here in Red Lodge. Grant came and offered his services in any way to help out. He was an artist and offered to upholster or do anything he could to help.

Q. Did you then meet Mabel Johnson? A. Yes, I did.

Q. How would you characterize their relationship?

A. I thought it was rather strange; not a normal mother-son relationship.

Q. Did you visit the home where Mabel Johnson and Grant Hamilton lived?

A. Many times.

Q. In the times that you visited their home did you have an opportunity to sit around and visit and talk?

A. I had dinner there several times.

Q. During those times did Grant ever go out to have a drink while you were there, or did you come after he had gone out for a drink?

A. Occasionally, I visited Mabel alone.

Q. Did Mabel Johnson have a temper?

A. Yes, she did.

Q. Did you observe Mabel Johnson and Grant Hamilton argue or fight?

A. I was there for a few arguments.

Q. What did they usually argue about?

A. His drinking or his taking money or not accounting for money or something.

Q. Did she expect him to account for the money he made to her?

A. Oh, yes, yes.

Q. Did he ever withhold some and get in trouble?

A. Quite frequently as a matter of fact.

Q. And she would get very angry?

A. Yes.

Q. She expected a full accounting of any money he had?

A. She felt he owed her everything he made.

Q. In the times that you visited them did you ever know Mabel to call a bar and try to find Grant?

A. Yes, she would find out if he was there and try to get him to come home. If that didn't work, she would personally go get him.

Q. You were close and were more family to both of them?

A. To both of them; I loved them both.

Q. When there was a dispute, who usually started it?

A. She did.

Q. Did you ever observe Mrs. Johnson call her son by Budd's name? A. On one occasion I can recall distinctly when I was singing at the Golden Eagle. They both came in very happy, drinking, both a little loose, and having a good time. It might have been a slip of the tongue but she did call him Budd.

Q. Did she help him with his drinking problem?

A. No. She would talk like she was going to but then she would go and buy it.

Miss Johnson: You may examine.

The Court: Mr. Ayers?

CROSS EX AMINATION OF BARBAR A RYAN BY MR. AYERS:

Q. Mr. Hamilton and Mrs. Johnson came into the Golden Eagle together?

A. Yes, they did.

Q. And sat down in a booth or something?

A. They were dancing.

Q. How did you happen to hear her call him Budd?

A. Well, I was actually interviewing for a job. I came in to sing a few songs and then when I finished, I sat down with them.

Q. And you say you first met Mr. Hamilton when you were at the Soup Shack; is that correct?

A. Right.

Q. And what sort of an organization was it?

A. It was a group of Christians and we gave shelter, hot homemade soup, and fried bread to the needy. We mostly remodeled it and got it started then it went financially under.

Q. And from time to time you noticed arguments developing between Mrs. Johnson and Mr. Hamilton?

A. Yes, on occasion.

Q. And it takes two to argue, does it not?

A. Yes.

Mr. Ayers: Thank you, nothing further.

Miss Johnson: The defense calls Todd Clark.

DIRECT EXAMINATION OF TODD CLARK BY MISS JOHNSON, MR. KAMPFE'S ASSISTANT:

Q. How long have you lived in Red Lodge, Todd?

A. About five years.

Q. Do you go to high school here?

A. Yes.

Q. What year are you?

A. Freshman.

Q. In the time that you have lived in the Red Lodge area, did you get to know Mr. Hamilton?

A. Yes.

Q. Did you also have an opportunity to meet his mother, Mabel Johnson?

A. Yes.

Q. What did you call her?

A. Mabel.

Q. Do you have a nickname or anything that you gave her?

A. Well, between Mr. Hamilton and I, when we were alone, we called her the warden.

Q. What have you always called Mr. Hamilton?

A. Ed.

Q. When you first met the two of them were you aware of their relationship; that he was her son?

A. For about a month nobody told me they were mother and son. I thought they were husband and wife.

Q. During the time that you knew them, did you stay overnight?

A. Yes.

Q. Was there one summer when you spent more time with them?

A. Yes. My mom and dad were living out of town and I was working in town, so I stayed with them.

Q. How old would you have been then?

A. About 12.

Q. Did Ed have a quick temper?

A. He might have but I have never really seen him blow up.

Q. Did his mother, Mabel, have a temper?

A. Yes.

Q. Did you ever see her blow up?

A. Yes.

Q. What did she blow up about?

A. At me or him.

Q. What would make her angry at you?

A. Work that I did wrong around the house and stuff like that.

Q. Did she yell?

A. Oh, yes. Told me that I was doing wrong and yelling.

Q. Did she yell at Ed?

A. Oh, yeah.

Q. When you stayed there, if Ed went out, did she ever call around town looking for him?

A. The first place she would call would be Newman's bar. Q. Did she get upset because of his drinking?

A. Yes.

Q. If he didn't want to come home from the bar, what did she do?

A. She'd slam the phone down and storm around a little bit and then if he didn't come home, she would go up there and get him.

Q. When she'd get angry with Ed when you were staying there, how did that make you feel?

A. Like sinking into the floor.

Q. Did she embarrass you then?

A. Well, I could tell Ed wanted her to put it off until later but she wouldn't stop, and I could tell that embarrassed him and kind of made me feel uncomfortable.

Q. Did he take orders from her?

A. Uh-huh.

Q. Did she give orders a lot?

A. Uh-huh.

Q. Was she dominating?

A. Very.

Q. Did he ever defy his mother; did he ever say no?

A. No, not just come right out and say no.

Q. Did Mabel drink at all when you had a chance to observe?

A. Yes.

Q. Did she keep any liquor around the house?

A. Yes.

Q. Did Grant ever raise his voice at his mother?

A. No, I can't ever remember him yelling at his mom. I can remember him just shooting little remarks but never raising his voice.

Q. Did Ed ever comment that he had a little money and perhaps he didn't turn it over to his mother?

A. Oh, I can remember one time; we were just riding around in the truck and he asked me if I wanted something to drink, and I said, "You know," and he just said, "Well, I have got a little money I didn't turn over to Mabel."

Q. Did you ever observe her hit or strike Ed?

A. One time I remember her slapping at Ed and missed.

Q. Would you tell me the circumstances of that?

A. She was in a bad mood that day anyway. She was yelling a lot so Ed took me and my little sister, and we went for a ride. We just drove around the country a little bit and looked around, and on our way back, we stopped at Newman's; he had a beer and we had a Pepsi.

Q. Go on?

A. We were playing pinball, pool, and stuff; then we went home and she just jumped all over him and said something about smelling his breath. He got close to her and she slapped him. Ever since then I remembered that one. It seems like I have seen her shove him or slap him a couple more times than that.

Q. Did Mabel tend to boss Ed around?

A. Uh-huh.

Q. And when she'd do that, he'd just take off?

A. Well, yeah, he wouldn't fight her back.

Miss Johnson: You may examine.

The Court: Mr. Ayers?

CROSS EXAMINATION OF TODD CLARK BY MR. AYERS:

Q. When you weren't staying with Ed and Mabel, who would you usually stay with?

A. My mom and dad.

Q. And who are they?

A. Barbara Ryan is my mom and I don't know where my dads at.

Q. Your mother testified just before you got here?

A. Yes.

Q. You stayed there with her permission?

A. Yes.

Miss Johnson: I have another question, Todd.

Q. Would you say that Ed and his mother got along better, for example, when they were drinking together?

A. Uh-huh.

Q. Was that about the only time they seemed to get along?

Miss Johnson: Thank you, Todd.

Witness excused.

DIRECT EXAMINATION OF MAE JORDON* BY MISS JOHNSON, MR. KAMPFE'S ASSISTANT:

Q. How long have you lived in RedLodge?

A. Seventy-one years.

Q. During those seventy-one years did you become acquainted with the defendant, Edwin Grant Hamilton?

A. Yes, I did.

Q. Did you also become acquainted with his mother, Mabel Johnson?

A. Yes, I did.

Q. Under what circumstances did you meet them, or can you recall?

A. Oh, I remember Mrs. Johnson when she was in high school; then when Grant was a little boy, he used to play with the little neighbor girls. He was a first grader or something like that.

Q. At that time, did he live with his mother?

A. He was with his grandmother and grandfather.

Q. Do you know how, at that time, he felt about his mother?

A. No, I don't but he was a nice child. Very nice child.

Q. In the latter years did you have an opportunity to become acquainted with Mr. Hamilton and Mrs. Johnson in another connection?

A. Mabel moved near me when Grant was about fifty.

Q. About how many years ago was that?

A. About four or five years.

Q. During that time did you have the opportunity to observe the two of them together?

A. Oh, yes. Practically every day I came in contact with them.

Q. Did Grant Hamilton ever have a temper?

A. No, I have never seen him with a temper. He was a very gentle person; very gentle.

Q. Did you ever observe Mabel Johnson angry with the defendant?

A. Oh, yes, I have; many times.

Q. How did he react?

A. He usually turned his back and walked away. He never abused his mother, never said an ill word to her; never.

Q. Did he ever argue back?

A. No, he would try to defend himself but he would turn his back and walk away.

Q. Did you know Mabel Johnson to ever take a drink?

A. Oh, yes. Mabel would take a drink, yes.

Q. Did you ever know Grant Hamilton to take a drink?

A. I really couldn't say I have seen Grant drink. I have seen him in the house and knew he wasn't supposed to, but he would serve a drink when his mother asked him to. In fact, I even had one with them.

Q. Did you know Grant to have a drinking problem?

A. Yes, I did. I knew he had a drinking problem and I really felt sorry for him because he didn't seem to have anyone to help him.

Q. Did Mabel Johnson help Grant with his drinking problem?

A. No, I don't think she did because when Grant came home different times, he'd have been hospitalized and he was ready to quit, but Mabel would have drinks in the fridge, or go down and get it, or have Grant go down and get it. I would say to her, "Don't do that, that's the worst thing on earth." She would say, "Well, if he can't handle it now, he never will." Well, he had no chance.

Q. Did she boast to you about the manner in which she treated her son?
A. Did she boast, did you say? No, she didn't boast although she told me things when Grant had his nice little upholstery shop. When Grant would have a few drinks too many, why, she would get mad and go out and sell his machines, and leave him without his tools.

Q. Did she sell his upholstery machines?

A. Yes, she did. She sold them twice and my husband asked her not to do that.

Q. Do you know why she did it?

A. Just because she was mad.

Q. Did Grant, to your knowledge, ever do some leather work?

A. Yes, Grant did leather work. In fact, I have a wallet I bought from him many years ago.

Q. Do you know what happened to his leather working tools?

A. His mother sold them. She just cleaned them out.

Q. Do you know the circumstances?

A. No. She told me about it though and that's when I said, "I don't think you are doing the right thing. Every time you get mad and Grant has one too many, you clean everything out that he has."

Q. Did Grant ever do any upholstery work for you?

A. Yes, he did it as a gift to me because I'd helped him a little one time, showed him pointers on it. And when my husband was dying; well, he had cancer of the lungs and he couldn't breathe too good. Grant made three beautiful cushions; hard ones for a brace to hold him up in.

Q. Did Mrs. Johnson ever discuss where she got her money?

A. Oh, yes. Now, at times Grant gave her every cent he would make on his upholstery because they were buying the material as they went along. It would have to be paid for and anything that was there, he would give his mother. I know that because she told me, and I was there when he gave her his checks.

Q. Did you have an opportunity to observe her exhibit any temper?

A. Directed to Grant, yes. Well, she had her house insulated and she had a little bad luck with it; it all came down and she called me on the phone, and I tell you, she just ripped me up and she ripped Grant up. I knew her temper; I just ignored it, but she gave it to Grant and he was trying to clean it up with his hands and everything else. Running to clean this insulation up.

Q. What was her reaction?

A. She was all but tearing her hair out, just raising cain, and he helped her with it. It came down a second time and she called me again, and I went down. It was the same thing. I don't know how Grant stood it.

Q. Did she ever talk to you about who bought Grant Hamilton's wardrobe?

A. Oh, yes. She used to buy him clothes and then he would buy his own too. She would give him the money to go down but Grant never had much chance. She would go down and choose his clothes, and she chose him nice clothes.

Q. Did you ever know the defendant to start an argument with her? A. No, I never did.

Q. Did you know of the relationship between Joanne Lahti and the defendant?

A. I knew she was going with Grant, and he couldn't have found a nicer girl; very lovely girl.

Q. Did Mabel tell you how she felt about Joanne?

A. She did one time. She said she was a Catholic and she didn't like that. Otherwise, she didn't object to their relationship.

Miss Johnson: You may examine.

The Court: Mr. Ayers?

CROSS EXAMINATION OF MAE JORDON BY MR. AYERS:

Q. You testified that Mrs. Johnson had a fiery disposition?

A. Yes.

Q. And she was like a firecracker. What sort of things would set her off?

A. Anything, just anything. Just something happens not to suit her.

Q. Did you ever see her set off like that because of Grant's drinking?

A. No, I didn't. She would say she didn't like it but she would never say too much to me because I said to her, "You are the one to blame for this because when the boy comes home and doesn't want to drink, you put it there."

Q. How would you describe Mrs. Johnson as being concerned with her appearance?

A. She was very vain and she liked to have herself done up well. Q. She was very meticulous, wasn't she?

A. Oh, yes.

Q. And very fussy about how she looked when she was out in public?

A. Oh, yes. Oh, yes.

Q. Or when she was with friends or neighbors?

A. Oh, yes, you bet she was. And she liked Grant looking nice and she kept him looking nice, too.

Q. Did you ever know her to decline going out in public unless she was made up, her hair fixed, and properly attired?

A. No. She was always dressed and clean, but I wasn't around her much when she went out. She and Grant used to go out on Saturdays and she would sometimes run in and let me see her; she was always dressed nice.

Q. Did Mrs. Johnson say that the only reason that she didn't like Miss Lahti was because Miss Lahti was a Catholic?

A. That's right.

Q. Do you find that particularly unusual that a person of this generation might still have some preferences as to what religion their children are into?

A. Oh, I think that will never end.

Q. That's common?

A. That's common, yes.

Q. Unfortunately?

A. Yes, it is very unfortunate.

Mr. Ayers: Thank you. Nothing further.

Witness excused.

DIRECT EXAMINATION OF MARION DAY* BY MISS JOHNSON, MR. KAMPFE'S ASSISTANT:

Q. Mrs. Day, how long have you lived in RedLodge?

A. Oh, about sixty years.

Q. During those sixty years did you have an opportunity to become acquainted with Grant Hamilton and his mother, Mabel Johnson?

A. Yes, ma'am I have.

Q. Approximately how many years ago would that have been?

A. Oh, between 1955 and 1960.

Q. How did you become acquainted?

A. They had a little gift shop in Red Lodge and so naturally I would go pick up gifts when needed.

Q. At the time that you met Mrs. Johnson and Mr. Hamilton, was Mrs. Johnson married?

A. She was married to Budd Johnson.

Q. Was he also involved in the gift shop?

A. Yes, he had a fix-it shop and she handled the gift shop, and Mr. Hamilton did leather work.

Q. Did he do your purse?

A. Yes.

Q. Did you ever do any work for them?

A. I did do some lacing.

Q. For example, did you do it on your particular handbag?

A. Yes, I did.

Q. During the time you were doing lacing for them did you have an opportunity to go to the shop on many occasions, or did you work at the shop?

A. No, I didn't work at the shop. I picked up the work and did it at home in my spare time.

Q. And how often did you do that, approximately? A. Oh, I may have laced 20 or 30 purses.

Q. When you were there did you have an opportunity to observe Grant and his mother together?

A. Not too often in front, at the counter.

Q. Did you go in back and talk with them?

A. Mabel would pick up the work from Grant and bring it out. On rare occasions, I went back. I didn't know Grant too well at the time because he was very quiet and gentle; I just didn't get to know him too well.

Q. What kind of impression did she give you of her son?

A. I would say, in my presence, she treated him like a child instead of of a full-grown man.

Q. Did she ever give you the impression that perhaps mentally he was a little deficient?

A. She treated him as though he didn't have any mentality.

Q. Did you observe whether or not Mabel Johnson had a temper?

A. Terrible temper.

Q. What would she do?

A. Oh, her language was just bad and she would throw things and go into tantrums.

Q. At Grant?

A. Anybody near her.

Q. Would she say anything to him?

A. Curse him.

Q. For example what? We will excuse you for saying it.

A. Oh, goddamn you, Grant.

Q. Did he ever mouth back at her?

A. In the time that I had business dealings with them, either in my home or at the shop, he never ever said a mean word to her or to anybody.

Q. How did Budd Johnson, Mabel's husband, react to this?

A. He did not like it. One day she had one of those tantrums; she was raising particular cain with her son when I went in to pick up a purse. Budd was so embarrassed. He just shook his head and said, "I have a notion to walk out that door, get in my jeep, and never come back."

Q. During the years, did Grant ever do any kind of work for you?

A. Yes, he has. In fact, a year ago he done some upholstering for me on a couple of chairs, and he also done some carpeting for me.

Q. When you paid for this did you make a check out to Grant? A. No, he told me I'd have to pay his mother for it.

Q. In their relationship would you characterize either of them as the boss?

A. She was the tyrant.

Q. Did Grant take to the subservient role?

A. Oh, yes. It was as though he had been beaten over and over. When she started coming near him, he'd go like this (indicating) and start ducking.

Q. How would you characterize Mabel Johnson?

A. I would say this; no one would ever be able to please her.

Q. Did you ever observe Grant having a temper?

A. Never, never in my presence.

Q. During the time you were at the shop did you ever observe Mabel Johnson throwing things?

A. She was always throwing things.

Q. Like what would she throw?

A. I brought back some left-over lacing one time. She went into a tantrum and just threw it towards him. He was in back of the store. It was embarrassing to be around her.

Q. During the time that you have known both Mabel Johnson and Grant Hamilton, would you say that either of them were friends of yours?

A. Well, what do you mean by friends?

Q. Did you associate with them?

A. Business wise, yes, and I liked dealing with Grant.

Q. Then how would you characterize the relationship between Grant and his mother?

A. Over the period of years I thought it was a poor relationship; she picked and picked and picked for no reason that I could see.

Q. Then you thought he was harassed?

A. Definitely.

Miss Johnson: Mr. Ayers, you may examine.

CROSS-EXAMINATION OF MARION DAY BY MR. AYERS:

Q. Mrs. Day, Miss Johnson did ask you whether or not you ever socialized with them and I assume from your answer that it would be no?

A. Well, yes, it would be no. I mean, we never partied together or had dinner at each other's homes.

Q. It was mostly business dealings?

A. Right.

Q. And that would be in connection with the leather work?

A. Yes, and that was many years ago. Recently I needed some carpeting and upholstery done, and Grant did that.

Q. Did you associate with Mrs. Johnson in the carpeting or upholstery work?

A. I would have to call her to get ahold of him.

Q. Right, but the business dealings were with Mr. Hamilton in that connection; is that correct?

A. Oh, she kept track of him every moment.

Q. But I mean as far as your dealings went, they were with Mr. Hamilton?

A. Except I had to pay her when it was a big job.

Q. How long has it been since you have been doing any lacing on the leather work?

A. Oh, I haven't done lacing for twenty-some years.

Q. I see. So other than the upholstering and carpeting that Mr. Hamilton has done for you, you've had no other connection with either he or Mrs. Johnson in the last twenty years?

A. Oh, I would see them when he done work for me.

Q. What sort of work, Mrs. Day?

A. Well, some yard work. I trim my trees and Grant came along and hauled the stuff away; little jobs, you know, that needed to be done.

Q. Did Mrs. Johnson come and help?

A. She came a few times with him but she didn't help him at all.

Q. She came a few times with him but she didn't help him at all?

A. Uh-huh.

Q. Would she come into your house and sit and watch him?

A. Not during the carpeting, no. He came by himself, but she would check in on him every little while; she was checking about something constantly.

Q. But as far as your actual personal contact with Mrs. Johnson, except for the carpeting, the upholstery, and some yard work, that would be about it; is that correct?

A. That's about it. We were not enemies; we talked when we met. But as I said, we didn't have much in common. Our mode of living was different.

Q. Now, you said that you never saw him drink; is that correct?

A. That's right.

Q. And if he did drink the reason, you didn't see him is because you only saw him when he was working; is that right?

A. That's right. He was always sober when I dealt with him, but I had never seen him drunk. When he came to work for me, he was always sober. The only thing that he drank was a cup of coffee.

Q. And he never drank any intoxication beverages in your presence?

A. No.

Q. Now, you said that nobody could really please Mrs. Johnson; is that right?

A. No. No, she was---

Q. She was really fussy about the way she looked?

A. The way she looked and everything she done in the shop. She was constantly fussing.

Q. I mean the way she had her hair fixed and the way she dressed?

A. Yes.

Q. Now, you say that when she would come near him, every time, he would sort of duck?

A. She would always have her little fists doubled up and I don't know why. She was so small, but she would double up her fists and curse and yell and rant.

Q. And that happened every time she came next to Grant?

A. Whenever he was around or whenever they were close together.

Q. And you never saw her any different than that?

A. No, he never spoke a mean word to her.

Q. Mrs. Day, you had an opportunity over the years to observe the quality of work that Mr. Hamilton did?

A. Yes.

Q. Did he do pretty good work?

A. Very good. Very nice to deal with.

Q. And he could turn out a sufficient amount of work?

A. Very good.

Q. Put in a full day?

A. Very good.

Q. And you say that Mrs. Johnson was very difficult to live with, in your opinion?

A. Yes, sir. Yes, sir.

Q. But that would be your opinion also that Mr. Hamilton could do sufficient work and of sufficient quality so that he could support himself without the aid of his mother; isn't that correct?

A. She wanted to domineer him.

Q. But he could if he wanted to; isn't that correct?

A. Probably could have. I don't know.

Mr. Ayers: I have nothing further.

Miss. Johnson: I have nothing further.

Witness excused

(The transcripts do not contain the attorney's closing arguments)

THE COURT ADDRESSES THE JURY:

You are instructed that when you retire, you are to elect one of your number as foreman and he or she will sign any verdict arrived at by the jury.

This being a criminal case, the verdict must be unanimous, which means that all of you must agree on the verdict.

You must find one and only one of the following verdicts:

1. Guilty of deliberate homicide

2. Guilty of mitigated deliberate homicide

3. Not Guilty

When you have reached a verdict, you will notify the bailiff, who will return you into Court. On September 14, 1978, the Jury had to make a decision based upon the following instructions:

A person commits the offense of criminal homicide if he purposely, knowingly, or negligently causes the death of another human being.

Criminal Homicide is mitigated deliberate homicide when a homicide which would otherwise be deliberate homicide is committed under the influence of extreme mental or emotional stress for which there is no reasonable explanation or excuse. The reasonableness of such explanation or excuse shall be determined from the viewpoint of a reasonable person in the actor's situation.

To sustain the charge of deliberate homicide, the State must prove the following propositions:

First: That the defendant on or about February 12, 1978, at RedLodge, Montana, performed the act or acts causing the death of Mabel Johnson; and

Second: That when the defendant did so, he acted purposely or knowingly.

If you find from your consideration of all the evidence that each of these propositions has been proved beyond a reasonable doubt, then you should find the defendant guilty.

If, on the other hand, you find from your consideration of all the evidence that either of these propositions has not been proven beyond a reasonable doubt, then you should find the defendant not guilty.

At 2:21 P.M. the jury retired to consider their verdict. At 4:30 P.M. the jury announced they were ready to deliver their verdict. At 4:37 P.M. the defendant and court officials heard the verdict.

VERDICT: We, the jury in the above-entitled action, find the defendant, Edwin Grant Hamilton, guilty of the offense of mitigated deliberate homicide.

CHAPTER 21

The Reckoning

My day of sentencing was set for September 28, 1978. The following is from the transcripts of those proceedings:

The Court: State versus Hamilton.

Mr. Kampfe: May it please the court that this is the time and place set for sentencing in this matter. I believe the Court has been fully advised of all the salient facts. The defendant testified during the course of his trial for approximately four hours. He went into the background of his life for you. In light of the rather exhaustive background information provided the Court, I believe the Court is in a position to properly pass sentence in this matter. I do not have any argument to present on behalf of the defendant.

Mr. Ayers: I agree with Mr. Kampfe that the facts surrounding this matter and the previous record of the defendant have been more than adequately presented to the Court, both through the defendant's testimony and the report of his previous records by the Department of Institutions.

Your Honor, in view of that past record and this tragic but heinous case and the circumstances surrounding it, it is the recommendation of the State of Montana that the defendant receive the maximum sentence permitted by law which is 40 years, and in addition thereto, may the Court impose a restriction which makes the defendant ineligible for parole and participation in the prisoner referral program.

The Court: Mr. Hamilton, would you please stand.

The Court: On September 14, 1978, you were found guilty of mitigated deliberate homicide. It is the judgement of this Court that you be and are hereby sentenced to serve a term of 35 years in the State Prison at Deer Lodge. So far as an order of this Court making you ineligible for parole or work furlough programs, the motion by the County Attorney in that regard is denied. I will leave that up to the discretion of the Board of Pardon and Parole.

The same day that I was sentenced, the sheriff flew me up to Deer-Lodge in my lawyer's airplane. I felt like jumping out of the plane and wished it would crash. If I'd flown by myself, I know I would have directed it right into the ground.

I was dressed like a Philadelphia lawyer, and was without handcuffs or restraints when we arrived at the Deer Lodge Airport. The guard, who was waiting for me, mistook the deputy sheriff for me because he was dressed in levis, rundown boots, and an old cowboy hat.

The guard said, "You are dressed up pretty nice to be coming to prison."

I told him, "It's old home week. I've been here before and want to make an impression on the boys."

They processed me in through the Maximum-Security Building which is about five miles from the old prison in downtown Deer Lodge. I was stripped and given a shower. It is normal routine to get sprayed with a delouser so I got the treatment even though I wasn't lousy. They checked all the cavities in my body for drugs or weapons then kept me in a maximum-security cell overnight. The next day, I was transported to the old prison in downtown Deer Lodge.

I'd lost all feeling and felt just like I was dead when my sentence was passed. That feeling lingered with me for several years after I was taken to prison. My first two weeks were spent on "fish row" where all prisoners start doing their time. We are kept isolated except for interviews, the mess hall, and showers. I fell right back into prison routine and felt that I'd eventually die there, and be laid to rest alongside some other convict I'd once helped bury; a pauper's grave in the unkempt part of the Deer Lodge Cemetery.

They pulled me off fish row because they needed an upholsterer who knew what he was doing. Right after that, I started attending Alcoholics Anonymous meetings. I spent almost two years in AA before I began reaching out and helping others; especially the younger guys who had alcohol and drug problems. After that I felt like I was really giving and doing something for others instead of taking.

I had many sleepless nights during those first two years. What I'd done to my mother ruled my conscience. Repeatedly, I would dream that I was free and that I'd met her someplace on the street. I'd tell her, "Tell those people you are not dead so they will turn me loose."

She'd laugh and say, "You got just what you deserved."

Then one morning I dreamt I was on a lonely stretch of sand by the ocean. In the distance, I could see a woman coming up the beach towards me. The woman was dressed up very nice and she was wearing a fur coat. My mother had always been a classy dresser and this woman looked like her. When she confronted me, I recognized my mother.

She told me, "Every night and every day, you have asked for my forgiveness. I forgive you and I love you." I threw my arms around her and woke up crying.

I had peace after that like a great burden had been lifted off me. After that dream, I felt different; life has been different. It was like being born again or the first day of my life.

The new prison was finished in 1979. I was put in handcuffs and leg chains then transported to my new home in a prison van. They put me in A-Unit which is a Medium One security building. Medium One prisoner is dressed out in khakis and they are not allowed outside the prison's security fence without handcuffs, leg chains, and a guard. A-Unit was completely opposite the old prison with its tiers, slamming doors, and concrete walls. Instead of an eight by four cell with steel bars, I had a bedroom of my own. I felt like I was turned loose. A-Unit was built like a large motel complex. Each section has a day room with a television set, a shower, and eight bedrooms. It seemed like the Holiday Inn to me. When the warden asked me what I thought of it, I told him, "When I woke up, I tried to find a sign telling when check-out time was."

The new upholstery shop wasn't finished so I applied for a job on the prison's paint crew. My boss told me that I should write a story about my life because she felt it was interesting. I said, "I can't write anything. Why don't you?" That's what started this story about my life.

While the pages of this book were being written there was considerable research being done by the author. She was able to acquire a (copy-1924) Greybull Standard which is Greybull, Wyoming's weekly newspaper. The front page carried a write-up about my father's death. He'd put a gun to his head and killed himself. I've actually been living a lie all my life because from the time I was old enough to understand, I was led to believe that he was killed by a dope addict. Mother always told me that he'd had a drinking problem and that she'd given him an ultimatum; he could either choose her or the liquor, so he quit drinking. Well, that wasn't the true story. She'd left him because of his drinking and went back to Red Lodge with me. All through the years, she'd hid this from me but I can understand her more now than I ever could. She passed on to me the very guilt she'd tried so hard to hide, and by doing so, she hurt me more than she helped me. I was deprived of my grandparents on my father's side; maybe today, I would be a physician instead of a convict if I'd been allowed to see them.

Perhaps if we could all be truthful with those we love, we could help form their life and possibly change it. Mine might have been changed if I'd known my father was an alcoholic. Even though he must have been a good doctor and surgeon, alcohol still destroyed his life and changed my own.

I've always been leery of drugs because I'd thought my father was killed by someone who desperately needed them. I may have abstained from alcohol or sought an answer to my addiction before it was too late.

I became involved with the Addictive Disease Studies Program while in Deer Lodge. This program was started when I was moved out from the old prison. I've seen so many so-called rehabilitation programs fail in State and Federal prisons. There is such a lack of trust between the prison population and the establishment. The ADSP was founded on the principles of Alcoholics Anonymous; like an alcoholic helps an alcoholic, the chemically dependent convict helps other chemically dependent convicts. The program is run by old cons like myself who have been around the horn, and are trusted by the other inmates. Young men coming into prison have a tendency to look up to the older convicts because they are accomplished safe-crackers, armed robbers, hit men, and counterfeiters.

They feel we can teach them a better way so they can get by with crime. But what they've never realized is that if we were so damn smart, why are we in prison? We decided to use their attitude in a positive way. The ADSP is designed to teach them a better way of life; how to stay out and stay clean.

The ADSP was given the green light by the prison's administrators.

It did not fail as they may have thought but has progressed. Right now, there are more convicts signed up for the program than can be accepted.

With the therapy groups limited to ten men and a prison population of over seven-hundred, it is impossible to reach everyone. A very careful selection is made among those who want to work in the counseling and guidance part of this program. They must be dedicated men who are tired of doing time. So many young convicts are looking for answers or solutions to their problems, and have no one to turn to or trust. They have received the ADSP with open arms. That trust would be gone if the administrative officials worked in the program. Mary Helen McCaskill, an alcohol and drug counselor, works with the program and she has been accepted by all who know her. She is dedicated and the convicts know this.

The Parole Board and the Department of Institutions have made the ADSP a mandatory requirement for anyone with a drug or alcohol related crime. The only incentive in this program is the willingness to change one's lifestyle because the convicts can't earn good time by attending.

The only rehabilitation in prison is self-rehabilitation; the desire to be who you actually are and not the person you present to the world.

New doors have opened for me during the last two years. The Kalispel, Montana AA group arranged for me to appear at several of that area's schools to speak to their young people. It may have been a coincidence but my appearance was set for Mother's Day, 1982. You could have heard a pin drop when I finished my presentation by saying, "By the way, I killed my mother."

Associate Warden Pat Warnecke must have realized how dedicated I've become because he was instrumental in arranging my appearance as guest speaker at the Montana AA Convention, Thanksgiving Day, 1982. I received a standing ovation when my speech was over. I spoke on the need for a change in our correctional system concerning grugs and alcohol. The tremendous influx of young people coming into our prisons are there mainly because of a lack of knowledge on drugs and alcohol. I feel the general public needs to show concern with the needs of this country's youth. We need more communication between parents and children, and both must remember it's a two-way street. Alcohol and drugs are where sex was thirty years ago in the schools; sex education is now out in the open and drug and alcohol education is still kept under the table. Kids come to me after they would hear me speak and tell me that there is a definite lack of communication with their parents, and a real need for education on drugs and alcohol.

I hear these comments from parents too; "My kid doesn't have a problem. He just drinks a little bit," or "I'd rather have my kid smoke marijuana than drink." What they don't realize is that after he smokes so much marijuana, he doesn't get the high he first got, so the next step is snorting cocaine. Mainlining cocaine usually comes next.

In March of 1983, the prison authorized my release to Galen, Montana which is an alcoholic treatment facility. I was told that I'd get training so I could eventually become a counselor. That program never got off the ground while I was there but I did learn a great deal about myself and alcoholism. I kept hoping for placement in a halfway house after treatment at Galen, but there wasn't any place for me so I had to go back to prison. Although I'd met many nice people who were either there for treatment or came to attend AA meetings, and had their support, I was still in a very depressed mood.

The Parole Board and Pat Warnecke were still working on a release plan but the wheels of time moved slow. Finally, an interview was arranged for me with the administrator of Alpha House which is a pre-release center located in Billings, Montana. He and three of his assistants drove up to interview me. They felt that I was a special case and thought I'd be a good influence on the young men at Alpha House, and the Billings community.

July 15, 1983, I was taken to the bus depot in DeerLodge where I boarded the bus for Billings. I was scared to leave the prison when that time came. What was I going to do at my age? My first week there, I almost told them to take me back to prison because I couldn't handle it.

I've been at Alpha House for two weeks now, and those fears are subsiding. A Billings upholstery shop hired me and I attend AA meetings almost every night. I've been asked to speak to the students in my home town of RedLodge. The Carbon County newspaper is interviewing me for a feature story which will be quite different than the headlines I made when I killed my mother. Who says old dogs can't be taught new tricks? I can fetch as well as carry now.

Alpha House is an old, rundown, railroad hotel that's been renovated by the inmates who live there. It still needs a lot of work but it sure beats a thin mattress and a stone bunk. Almost all of the renovation materials have been donated; even most of the furniture. After much apprehension, Alpha House has been accepted and is showing excellent results. The public has a new awareness of the needs of men being released from prison.

Since a furniture store occupies the first floor of the hotel, Alpha House has the second floor. We all share a toilet and bath which is located half-way down a long hall. The kitchen is small but adequate. The staff eats with us in the dining room. When all twenty-five of us are present at mealtime, it is crowded. We have an older colored television which is hooked up to cable, in the dining room. A broken-down pool table that should be in the dump is located in the recreation room, but we aren't complaining because here is where we have a chance to adapt back into society. We are not thrust out into a world we've lost contact with. I can go downtown or to the bathroom without expecting a shake-down; I don't need anybody holding my hand now. The staff does a nightly bed check to be sure everyone is accounted for.

The average stay at Alpha House is six to nine months. We all have house chores like cleaning the bathroom, recreation room, etc., and we are responsible for our own rooms. Residents must pay three dollars a day until they find a job, then we are required to pay twenty percent of our gross monthly salary.

Besides my job and regular AA attendance, I've become involved in Twelve Step work. That is working with alcoholics who are having problems, and trying to help them find a better way of life. I have no degrees; the only one I have is a degree in life that can't be copied in any college, no matter what the course is.

There is a Higher Power or whatever you choose to call Him. I am dedicating this book to all the drunks and junkies who are wandering our streets or sitting in prison. May you find that Higher Power and free yourselves from an insane way of life. I hope that by reading this book just one person learns, listens, and changes their lifestyle. Then, I can say I've done one good thing in my life.